Let the rains Stop! Let the clouds Clear!
Open this cover and let the Sunshine in! Here is,

A Better Way!

DonRicardo G. Salazar

WESTBOW
P R E S S
A DIVISION OF THOMAS NELSON

WestBow Press books may be ordered through booksellers or by contacting:

WestBow Press
A Division of Thomas Nelson
1663 Liberty Drive
Bloomington, IN 47403
www.westbowpress.com
1-(866) 928-1240

Because of the dynamic nature of the Internet, any web addresses or links contained in this book may have changed since publication and may no longer be valid. The views expressed in this work are solely those of the author and do not necessarily reflect the views of the publisher, and the publisher hereby disclaims any responsibility for them.

Any people depicted in stock imagery provided by Thinkstock are models, and such images are being used for illustrative purposes only.

Certain stock imagery © Thinkstock.

ISBN: 978-1-4497-1464-2 (sc)
ISBN: 978-1-4497-1463-5 (e)

Library of Congress Control Number: 2011925489

Printed in the United States of America

WestBow Press rev. date: 04/01/2011

A Better Way!©

Today's Small Business Community of the United States, is Not the Small Business Community Model our Founding Fore-Fathers Created!

The following two *Mantras* are the two most basic building blocks in all theories on the concept of Improvement in the World of Business.

When the *Trials & Tribulations* of Life bring you to a screeching halt, try with every fiber of your being to remember these two basics. Brand them into your sub-conscious. They will provide you with hope again; the ability to dream again, to begin anew.

They may apply to both, your career and personal life. Your entire future may depend upon these two basics at your time of need, to pick you back-up and *want* to start again. Why?

If you tried it once, you'll know; they will never fail to give you the clarity you'll need.

If you want to know the Future, look at your past. If you see anything you don't like, you & Only You have the Power to change it!

Take the Substance of the past and combine it with the Light of the New. The Result will provide you with "A Better Way!" for your future

Author: DonRicardo G. Salazar ©2011

Contents

Introduction

Morgan Franklin Associates was founded on January 1, 2000.

As of January 2011, *Morgan Franklin Associates, Sales Management Consultants, AKA*, MFA Consultants, made *a commitment to donate a percentage of the profits, from the sale of our book, **A Better Way!,*** toward helping the **Small Business Community** make their come back.

We want this book to be more than a *ray of hope* but rather a *hand-up*, for all Small Businesses to use toward regaining their previous position. The position they held since our founding Fore-Fathers built it; known as, ***the Back-bone of the entire U.S. Economy, and we want it back, now!***

DonRicardo, G. Salazar, founder of MFA Consultants, took the advice of author, Ruth Stafford Peale's quote, ***Find a need and fill it.*** From, 2000 to 2010, MFA Consultants provided small and large Corporations with sound successful, consulting advice, based upon their respective needs, such as, *Start-up Corporations, Corporate Expansions and Crisis Management.*

However, economically speaking, we could see the writing on the wall. It was inevitable, that this downward spiraling Economy would place the Small Business Community first, on the hit-list of casualties. Today, we now know this to be true, ending with apocalyptic results on a National and Global level.

Well, we at MFA find this to be an unacceptable state of affairs! As it remains, it appears to be almost permanent, or possibly at a micro-degree of recovery at best. ***Well, not on our Watch!*** We had to help speed-up this recovery effort! So, as Founder of MFA, I decided to make some type of a positive difference. Therefore, we are making a two-fold contribution. First, we invested the last two years, designing and developing new, basic Sales Management Models, specifically designed for those areas we believe would best benefit the Small Business Community in regaining their losses, as quickly as possible.

In addition to placing the *unique Sales Management Models*, in our new book, specifically designed for the Small Business Community; we invested all our time, energy and monies, over the last two years, toward no other projects, than the creation and development of all new *Sales Management Models,* in order to assist the SBC recoup their losses that much faster. In that effort, we are targeting the bottom rung of the Sales Ladder and moving up through the ranks of Senior Sales-Management.

Included, are those *novice* Sales-Representatives and those newly appointed Sales-Managers, who until now, never had the opportunity to be professionally educated in the **Art of Selling.** I have personally met thousands with college degrees, just not in Sales & Marketing.

When you purchase this book, *A Better Way?*, you'll see it strategically focused on areas, most productive to recapture the quickest growth in new revenues for the Small Business Owners.

It is aimed at teaching *professional Sales-Structure Models,* to those who, recently secured a job they can feel passionate about, in the Sales Industry. But, like most new-hires, they feel if their Boss ever found out, just how little education they have in the *Art of Selling*, they'll be let go. And that same fear, applies to all those newly appointed Sales-Managers, lacking the same exposure.

These Small Business Owners, may ensure these new Sales-Tools are re-enforced, by taking our two-day Seminar for an in-depth study on the new methods of **A Better Way?** Your Sales teams will be ready to hit the streets running!

Dedications

I am compelled to say, without the love, loyalty and support of my beautiful and always youthfully, positive-natured wife, Miss Joanie, I would never have had the courage to put my pen to paper, for this book. She's believed in me, from the very beginning, thirty years ago, and continues to this very day.

She had the foresight to see *where,* there was a need, and felt that I *possessed the successful, positive accomplishments and experience,* to offer this group of businesses, *a hand-up,* in their effort to reclaim the status previously held within the *Small Business Community* of this great Country. This group covers, coast to coast and border to border, of our forty-eight contiguous United States, plus Alaska and Hawaii.

My wife was well aware of my concerns, over the past twenty-five plus years, of their declining position from the once, proudly held status, our *founding Fore-Fathers touted,* as *the Back-Bone of the United States Economy,* to an almost extinct, historical existence.

She gave me such an over due, *wake-up call,* I felt guilty by default, that I had not launched this undertaking years ago. For that, I shall be forever grateful.

Acknowledgements

They say, by the time you hit sixty years of age, you can count your best friends on one hand. I am proud to say, I need both hands. They go from fifty five to thirty years back!

Of those, there are seven gentlemen, of whom, repeatedly said of me; *one thing about Ricardo is a proven fact. When ever he is kicked by life's trials and tribulations, deserved or not. He always, gets back up, dusts himself off and starts his trek again; one step at a time and always rises back to a higher station in life, than before.*

You all have my undying gratitude for your continued support and sincerest loyalty: My Brother Ernest Salazar, Phil Catania, Dan Griffin, Bob Mullet and a special *Tip of the Hat*, to my very dear friends, Frank P. Morsilli, Michael Travis and Brandon Houston.

Preface

"I shall commit to donating a percentage of the profits from this book, towards helping the Small Business Community, where and when, I see an appropriate need."

…DonRicardo

Happiness is yours, if you find *Passion*, in your work.

I write this book, with the best of intentions; first, to assist all those people, who are trying to find *Passion in their Job*. If you are one of those people, out there still looking for it, do not stop. Be *persistent*! Never give up!

Nothing will bring you closer to achieving the goals you set in life than *persistence*! Not money and certainly not, high connections. Nothing brings you Success more than *steady persistence*! Never give up, *use persistence* until you have found your *Passion*! Keep looking! It might take you a day, a month, a year, but you will find it!

For me, I found *my Passion in Sales*, and in the journey I took, in learning the *Art of Selling*. There is no other feeling, compared to the pleasure you will receive, once you have found your own *Passion*, in life's work.

What do you enjoy? I mean, what do you feel, deeply *passionate* about? Boating, building Hot-Rods, Writing, or playing music? What ever, it is, *be persistent!* Find a way to get into that Industry. At first, you may have to take a position as an Intern, or an Apprentice, just to get into the industry where you can feel *Passionate* about your work. It's ok to take any job available within the industry you're *Passionate* about, just to get entry within that genre.

Then listen and learn, from your co-workers who have already gone down the same path, which you are now pursuing in that same industry. Ask them all the questions you can think of, every day. Don't be afraid to ask for Advise. People help those, who are sincere.

I had the pleasure of meeting, thousands of Novice Sales-Reps & New Sales-Managers within the *Small Business Community*, during the thirty years I spent globe-trotting, from city, to state, other countries, and back. One year after another. It was an experience of a lifetime. I did it with *Passion* and loved every second of it!

During all those years, I discovered an unbelievable, number of uneducated people, in the business of Sales, or Selling. Not to say they were without high school diplomas, college degrees, or even with Masters Degree's. I must say, the latter, were found to carry a Cavalier attitude, acting as though there was nothing more for them to learn in life. I quickly learned to thin the herd, and focused my energies upon those who showed a genuine positive attitude toward wanting to improve and enjoy the enrichment of their life's choice in Vocations.

These uneducated, only in the *true Art of Selling*, Sales-Reps were performing their duties poorly at best, through-out the National, and International Business Community. Like termites, creating chaos in every aspect of the Business. An uneducated Sales-Rep will cause irreparable damage in the process. Who's to blame? I say both, the Sales-Rep due to ignorance and the Small Business Owner for not investing in educating their Sales-Reps and Managers, are at fault!

They, were allowed go out, with out a clue, a plan, or direction! From anyone, at all! Absolutely, no support! No Guides, Daily Reports, or Weekly-Schedules. Nothing at all! Like giving Columbus ships with no sails, no rudders and crews with no experience in Sailing! Six months later, the Queen would be wondering, I gave him lots of Gold, how could he possibly fail? He probably fell off the edge of the Earth?

So, at the end of each month, or quarter, the Sales-Rep doesn't have a clue as to **who, where, when, why, how,** or **what,** may have caused this debacle. So, please, educate your self.

If you're the Owner, you should invest in some small way, to offer assistance, to your Sales Employees. Become honest and responsible owners and walk tall and proudly again, amongst your peers, with pride of ownership.

Re-invest in yourselves and your unique, Small Business by sending your Sales-Reps and your Sales-Managers to some good old fashion, How to… Seminars. You'll get it back, ten-fold, and put your Small Business on the map again! Give your Competition a strong shove back, to the end of the line. *Make it happen!*

So, Carpe' Diem, be Pro-active and Seize the Day!

Passion

On September 1, 2010 the results of a ten year study, was revealed by the United Press to alert the Public. The study was performed by Independent Specialists in Demographics. This study compared these startling results; from September 1, 2000 and September 1, 2010. The study question was: How many Americans are *happy* in their present Job? Results showed in the year 2000, there were **65%** of those employed, who stated they were happy in their chosen Professions.

Compared to the year 2010 results, showing only **43%** of those employed, were happy in their chosen fields. I found this to be a very sad testimonial of the times, to say the least. How can we alert the Business Community, no matter their size, about this declining ratio?

If they are serious about increasing the USA's Productivity by a significant margin, say **23%**, if only to reach the same level of ten years ago. Then please, I cannot turn this *Titanic* by myself. Everyone who reads this book must sound the alarm.

I feel like *Paul Revere*, riding alone in the night, shouting aloud, *read these statistics: Happy workers* **produce 33% to 50% more** *than unhappy workers!* Maybe they'll listen, if I shout aloud; *unhappy workers produce approximately* **33% to 50% less,** *than happy workers!*

Before I proceed to discuss the topic of *Sales, as a Profession*, I must first qualify my audience. If your, *true Passion,* is not in the World of Sales, I strongly suggest you stop reading this book any further.

Instead, I would prefer you gave this book, to some one you may know, who is *truly Passionate* about their job in Sales as their Vocation. They should be grateful, and who knows, they may return the favor in kind? If you do not feel Passionate in your work, then I strongly suggest, you leave immediately,…run,…do not look back!

As for those of you who *are not happy* in your field of work, write a list, with all things that you enjoy. Don't listen to your friends, family, or coworkers. Just listen to your own heart. Only you, know what truly pleases you. A job that provides you with a strong sense of accomplishment at the end of the day, every day! *Now that's Passion!*

You've heard, time after time, people saying, follow your dreams. Pursue your dreams, or you'll never find true happiness. Well, those people are absolutely *Spot-on*! Don't give up, keep searching until you find a job, that possesses those qualities which you can truly, be *Passionate and happy at work.* You remember the old saying; *if at first you don't succeed, try, try again! Now that's persistence!*

You'll see everything different from the very first day. There's an old saying; the last thing you want engraved on your tombstone are five words; *If only I had, tried?* My Father was one of those men. I saw him come home every day, with all those frustrations, mood swings, feeling hopeless about any possibility of change in his future. That was the *old guard.* Take the job you could get, work hard doing the same thing over and over for thirty years. *Get a gold watch and die.*

A healthy, highly intelligent, articulate individual's entire life wasted. He used to walk around, after some *opportunity for change* had passed him by,… too late. He would always say those five words,… *If only I had, tried?* In olden times, no one cared about being happy with what you did for a living. Only, the fact that you had a job, any job! Too many sheep, not enough creative thinkers asking themselves,…*what if I looked for employment in an industry I would really enjoy working at?* Sadly, too little too late! But not for you, no matter what your age!

I swore to myself, I'll never die with those feelings he harbored all those years. There was never a guaranty of success, but how much happier could he have been, *if only one possibility had worked out?*

Overview of *A Better Way?*

Now, I'm not claiming to be the *know all, be all Sales Guru.* I was just like a lot of you out there, who found themselves in Sales, and just started by placing one foot, in front of the other. Until I realized, I wasn't very successful due to my lack of education in the *Art of Selling.* So, after years of study, I created my own *MBO & ADEE Models* as a *basic How-to-Guide* for new Sales-Reps and Managers.

I purposely wrote this book in an abbreviated format, to pass on for you to use, as your building blocks, in the hopes of nurturing your fresh, open minds, to assist you in creating your own *Sales-Models*, based upon your own individuality. Your individuality will be developed through a combination of your applying my two *Sales-Models* with the practical knowledge base you develop by using your newly gained data from all customers. The good, the bad and the ugly!

The lesser status customers are perfect clay models for you to mold into greater revenue producers by using your new *MBO, Action-plans.* After you've digested the pertinent data retrieved from various interviews with your existing customers, competitors, superiors and peers. You may now apply this data in the creation and development of your own unique *MBO, Action-plans*, allowing you to surpass your monthly, quarterly and annual Sales Goals for the New Year.

So, please use this as your canvas, to create your own future, your own way. Create it to fit you, and you alone, and remember, this is not like those other, *How to make Billions, through Sales books*, that clutter the shelves, only to end up, in so many *used book* stores.

This book is a *Basic-Guide for beginners*, no more, no less. After studying these methods, I believe you'll be able to create the power necessary, to raise the Small Business Community up, again. Like a *Phoenix*, rising up from the ashes, to re-establish our Small Business Community back, to our envied status of old; the *strong Back-Bone* of the United States Economy, as it was before, on the global level.

The first of the two *Sales-Models* I offer in this book, *A Better Way*, is the *MBO, Management By Objectives Action-Plan*. This Model is targeting only the novice Sales-Representatives. They are created and designed to be simplistic and *basic Sales-Models*. I developed these Models in a fairly open format, thereby allowing you expand upon it with some experimentation, until you feel secure enough in your respective environment, to apply your own creativity, based upon your personal experience. And, as you mature from the novice status, on up to a well seasoned, Professional Sales Representative!

The *MBO Model*, is requiring you to be very pro-active and strong disciplined. I am compelled to remind you, that this book is only intended for those of you, who are seriously interested in improving your lot in life. This uniquely designed to be very short, simplistic, educational process should be a tremendous motivator! I am offering you a rare, **per value received, gift.** That is, when you are placed in an unexpected position of receiving, **more bang for the buck.**

I sincerely hope, all you Novices feel this way, three to six months, after applying the Models in your daily, weekly and monthly Action-plans, I know I did. So, I would appreciate you not including my book in the same category, as those *get Rich Overnight, fast talking, late night TV-Hawking, Super-Hero, Mega-Sales Persons!* No empty promises here, only the opportunity to improve yourself, through serious study, practical application in the Marketplace, and hard work.

However many books I read on different styles of Business Management, and there were copious amounts of them, they made it possible for me to pick and choose, very specific salient points, terminology and theories, for me to use like mortar in the building blocks of my own, creative thought process which gave birth to my own two beginner's Sales Models. Maybe, you can make a significant difference in our combined efforts toward raising the *Small Business Community, back to the powerful Backbone of the US Economy.*

As to the *second Model, the ADEE, Assessment, Development, Entry and Expansion,* is aimed at the newly appointed *Sales-Manager* and what they may expect in their newly appointed position of *increased Duties and expanded Responsibilities.* One statement the new Sales-Managers can expect to hear from their old Peers will be *that's why they get the Big Bucks!* They're not wrong, superior results will be expected from their former Peers and that will result in larger bonuses for the new Sales-Manager!

Again, the *ADEE Model* was specifically designed for the new Sales-Manager, who also, never received any exposure, to formal education in Sales & Marketing, Professional Sales-Seminars, or Home-studied courses on Management-Skills. Albeit, they may have attended some College; or even received their Batchelor's and Master's degree; only not in the area of their *Passion, in Sales.*

That's why this is targeting only those of you who are now ready to apply yourselves to learning, *Professionally, Structured Sales-Management Models* using these basics, as mortar, in building the necessary foundation blocks for creating the professional, regimented, pre-planned actions you need in order for you to develop competitive-proactive methods of providing your Boss, the Small Business Owner, with a quicker growth in new sales revenues, in addition to, garnering greater percentages of revenue from your Bosses top five Competitors, by winning over each of their top five Customers.

This process will become second nature to you, only if you are serious about becoming a real, Pro! I am writing this book to enlighten you on how to evolve from a Sales-Rep/Manager, working for a living, to a person who can make a very good living, while enjoying the journey during their working hours, in achieving their goals. All, the while assisting your Boss in the growth-process of their Company and enjoying every minute of each and every day. Where it is a true joy, to do what you do, by choice.

After studying this book and putting the respective *Models* into practice in the real world, I do believe, even the least educated, in the Sales Industry, combined with the direction and support you will receive by attending our Seminar, will gain the intrinsic value of an accomplished, well seasoned Professional in the Sales Industry.

Between the two, studying the book, combined with attending the Seminar, will fill you with pride, integrity and just the right amount of self-confidence about the ways of the world of Sales. For the first time in your Sales career, you will be able to walk side by side, along with the best, of the best!

From that moment on, you will have become a self-empowered individual who stands out from the crowd. A Sales Professional with a deep sense of knowledge within your own Industry and a very high degree of character which will intimidate all others, with less. All of these newly developed characteristics will be noticed and duly noted, by your Boss, the Owner, in the Small Business Community; including, your top Competitors.

What will be noticed first and foremost? What will be most evident, shall be the quantifiable healthy growth in your increased revenues. The new growth in revenues, plus the increased number of new customers will be jumping off the pages of your monthly and quarterly Aging reports!

Always remember and never forget; that *Aging Report*, is your Bible! You will live, or die by what it tells your boss every month and every quarter. Not only in gross sales dollars, but also in net profit dollars. These are determined by what your Sales-Price was to your Customer.

The *Aging Report should also be your Bible!*

Why is this so important? Because, if you cut your price only to move more product, thereby increasing your gross sales dollars, you may have put the Bosses Small Business in the Red, for that month, or worse yet, for the entire Sales Quarter. How could that have happened? By not verifying your sales price from your Boss prior to quoting a number you gave the Customer, so you would get the order. **Priorities!** You must learn to keep your *priorities* in order at all times.

First *priority*: If you sell a widget, it must be sold at a profit. This must *always* come *prior* to your hitting your gross monthly sales, or quarterly goals! Keep in mind, should you make such a mistake, and it is a large one, it won't be just *your* job in jeopardy, but it could cause a negative effect on your Bosses Business. It could hurt the business in such a way it would not be able to recover overnight. It could take a year or more. That means your Peers, fellow Sales-Reps, Customer-Service and Shipping Personnel may have to be laid-off. Not just you. So, keep your priorities straight and in order at all times. Believe me, such short-sided incompetence is *never* acceptable and you would be *fired, let go, or Persona Non Gratis, immediately!*

More lessons like those listed above, shall be incorporated throughout the following chapters. However, we will attempt to place, at least one full page, or rather a dedicated list of lessons, for you to use as needed, for reference material in your efforts toward improving the future results of your respective *Aging Reports;* especially the *Year-To-Date,* final *Year-End, Aging-Report!*

Before moving on to the *MBO, Management by Objectives Sales Model,* and the *ADEE, Assessment-Development-Entry & Expansion, Action-Plan Model,* I want to assure our readers, we did our best to keep any unnecessary minutia, out of this book. You're already in the work force; now you require a more myopic approach in your career, targeting your focus on spending the rest of your working years on the edification of the Industry of your *Passion, Sales,... **A Better Way.***

MBO, Basic Model for Novice Sales-Reps

This, chapter, is mainly intended for the **Novice Sales-Rep.** One who has never been taught a *structured, basic, How-to, Sales Guide.* Once you have studied these basics, it is imperative to start as soon as possible, for you to apply these newly learned *Action-Plans,* into your every day work schedule, the sooner the better.

The sooner you incorporate these *Action-Plans* into your daily *MO, Method of Operation* the better. With each day that passes, your newly developed *MO* becomes second nature to you. After about six months you shouldn't have to think about your *Methods of Operation* again. By then, they should be etched into your memory-banks, *forever!*

With out an education in Sales, your success will be limited. You'll need at least, a modicum of exposure to a structured Sales Model. So I developed a basic MBO format, if only to give them a *jump-start,* into the embryonic stages of a structured Guide, to help them get started.

After three months, of serious disciplined, adherence, of using this basic guide. You'll be able to incorporate some of your own personal traits into your daily activities. This *MBO* was designed to be malleable in that regard, so as to make an easy transition for you.

MBO: *Management by Objectives:*

Is an *Action-Plan-Outline,* for Sales-Representatives to use in developing their Goals, Objectives and Missions to process their daily work-schedule with a modicum of professionalism, in order to enhance the personal style of your daily work. Also, this *MBO* will allow you to expedite the number of existing and potential Customers you see each day, thus maximizing your *MTD, Month to date,* results.

How prepared you are in advance, *will* stand out. Your Superiors are looking for these signs. It shows them who, in their *Stable of Sales-Reps,* is showing signs of promising professional growth. These methods alert them, as to who is truly serious, about their work and who is not. Believe me you will never go without a structured Action-Plan, again. It will separate you from the rest of the herd.

You know, you've seen those haphazard Reps, who go out every day, with no plans what so ever, as to where they are going, or who they are going to visit that day, or any other day. Why? Because, it's only a job to them, and not a *Passionate Career!* I would like say, an 8:00am to 5:00pm day. But realistically, you and I both know better. Realistically, it's more like a 10:00am to 4:00pm day, at best.

Again, I say, why? Because, they have no Passion for the work they are performing, it's ***just a Job*** to them. You can spot them in the middle of a crowd. The only thing you can count on this type of Sales-Rep, is their monthly Sales performance. Their *Month To Date,* results will always be **consistently, inconsistent!** And a very short list of long-term Customer relationships! *You can take that to the bank!*

I am sure there are several *well seasoned,* Sales-Reps, due to a lack of an education in Professional Sales, who still go out, first thing Monday morning of every week, without a single idea, of **w**here, **w**hat, **w**hen, **h**ow, or **w**ho, they are going to call on, that very day. Much less, what their daily goals are. And, more than likely apply the same unknown travel itinerary, through the rest of the year.

Shame on them and shame on their Bosses! I am not chastising them for being uneducated. Their ignorance is only due, to the lack of having been taught any formal methods of how to improve themselves, toward becoming a Professional, Sales Representative. But, this is their **Wake-Up Call!** These *SBC Owners* should invest in educating their respective Sales Representatives! They won't regret it.

Maybe, it's just what the Doctor ordered; you study hard and apply all the recommendations I have placed in this Book. Maybe, it will take you, all the way to the top. As for me, personally, the *Top* has never been what I have aspired to reach. *You'll know* when you found the appropriate level that is *your personal* Comfort Zone.

These are the *Basics*. I developed these *Basics* over a period of thirty years in the *World of Sales;* during which, I learned from the Best, at five different multi-billion dollar Manufacturing Corporations. I would not write, nor recommend these methods, if they hadn't already proven to be extremely successful for me in the past. I can honestly say if they don't help improve your Sales, you're definitely not applying them correctly. Why? Because I have trained, and mentored over 1,600 Sales-Representatives, and I'm still batting 1,000%!

In time, should you change Industries, you'll be able to go back and refer to this book. Review it and again, re-apply the same basics to that new Industry, until you are able to redesign your own unique *MO*, for that respective industry. It worked for you before; it will again!

MBO, Action-Plan

MBO, Management by Objectives in it's most basic form

First, you *set your Goal* for the *New Year's Annual Gross Sales.*

How? There are two methods of determining this amount:

First, some Companies give you a mandated number, which is typically 10%-12% more than you produced the prior year. This is typical of the average Lazy Sales-Manager, who doesn't want to perform their due-diligence. This may sound like the easier of the two, but a more in-depth method makes you a more prepared and valuable Professional Company Sales-Rep.

First example:

2009, you produced $1,000,000 in gross sales.

2010, you must reach $1,100,000 to $1,120,000 gross sales.

($1,000,000 x 110%, or 112% = New Years gross sales.

The Second method requires much more scrutiny on your part by using an in-depth study of your prior year's *Quarterly Aging-Reports.*

You must break down each quarter by Rep, by Customer, by Product(s) and by Gross Profitability, in each category listed. How?

Second example (A):

Look up your highest, purchasing Customer by dollar volume.

Compare their results in 2009's first quarter, to their second quarter, to their third quarter and their fourth and final quarter's results:

ABC Plumbing Supply's:

1st: $875,000   2nd: $988,750   3rd: $1,166,725   4th: $1,423,405
                (+ 13% growth)   **(+ 18% growth**   **(+ 22% growth)**

Total Annual Gross Sales for 2009 = $4,453,880 or a 510% growth for 2009. That's an average of 17.7% growth over three straight quarters.

Now, to determine what those same results show over four quarters for 2009, you would have to average a 12.8% growth over each of the four quarters. That 12.8% growth per quarter, compounded, is what you must grow at no less than a 16% growth compounded, for each of the four quarters of 2010, in order to show you're worth your salt.

Second example (B):

Now you review the *Profitability-Factor.* Your, *Aging-Report* will also show ABC's list of products purchased and at what price they paid, after all their appropriate discounts. This is when you must rely on your Sales-Manager disclosing what percentage of profit is acceptable, for each product purchased. Keeping in mind, their discounts, based on quantities purchased and shipping costs.

Setting your discount structure; your initial discount structure is based on how much your Customer purchases each year. Historically, ABC Company has proven to be a large Customer. What about the lesser purchasing Customers? I found, as a Manufacturer, to always minimize the variables when ever possible; and this is a perfect area to apply it. I prefer to keep your basic discount structure down to three levels; no more than four.

Second example (C):

Bronze level discount Customers   - **Silver level** discount Customers
50/10/2% = 56% net discount   50/25/2% = 63.25% net discount

Gold level discount Customers   - **Platinum level** discount Customers
50/25/10/2% =67% net discount   - 50/25/10/5/3/2%=70% net discount

Platinum level, ABC, Co.: 50/25/10/5/3/2% = a 70% net discount or they are basically paying 30.5 cents on every dollar *of your list price*. Why would you ever give such a great big discount for your largest Customer, like ABC Company, when they are only spending $4.5 million a year on your products? My reason is because that $4.5 million only represents that Company's purchases for the Western Region. They also buy for three more regions in the USA, plus Canada and Mexico. Total annual purchases = $18 million per year.

In addition to a *Platinum* account's large amount of purchases, they also have 600 showrooms with a minimum of twenty five of our products on display in each showroom. Additionally, this account has five stocking-warehouses, with a minimum of 200 products, already purchased, in-stock.

A break down of the *Platinum* discount is:

50% off list pricing = 50€ on every dollar at list price.
Plus 25% off the 50€ = 37.5€ on every dollar at list price.
Less 10% off the 37.5€ = 33.75€ on every dollar at list price.
Minus 5% off for being an *International* account = 32€ " " " .
Less 3% for a year-end annual *rebate for damaged goods* = 31€ " " .
Less 2% quick-pay discount *if paid within ten days* = 30€, " " .

That leaves you the Manufacturer, with 45% GP, Gross Profit =13.5€ cents out of every 30€ the Platinum customer spends on our products.

As a manufacturer your *CODB*, Cost of Doing Business = 75% (10€):

CODB includes such cost factors as: Manufacturing of products, Research & Development for the products, machinery, packaging, shipping, rent for office facilities, and or, manufacturing plant, utilities, security and all personnel involved. Plus the Marketing tools, brochures, mailers, catalogues, advertising, conventions and the respectable personnel.

Including the above, are the Sales costs, salaries, commissions, bonuses and their related expenses, company cars, auto-insurance, fuel, maintenance and depreciation; plus all fixed assets, desks, computers, telephones, copiers, fax machines, company cell phones and office personnel, warehouse/shipping personnel, including management, middle-management, junior, senior and all executives.

Your EBIT, or Earnings Before Interest & Taxes = 25% of the GP, or 3.5€ = a very respectable percentage of **net profit, or net-net!**

The Platinum customers give the manufacturer the lowest amount of ROI, Return on Investment, and the least percentage of profit per sale.

However, these contracts do provide you, the manufacturer, a more than acceptable amount of ROI, and (%) of profit. But the true quantifiable value is the guaranteed flow of cash, or monthly revenue they produce, which satisfies, slightly more than necessary in surpassing the monthly CODB, Cost of Doing Business.

There by freeing-up more quality time for the entire Sales/Marketing Team to focus on the more profitable sales. From enhancing the annual gross sales from your *smaller Bronze and Silver accounts*, to the more *profitable product offering*, which contains a much greater percentage of profit, built into the pricing structure.

It is in the journey of finding that perfect combination of efforts by all, where the *Passionate Sales personnel* find their intrinsic-valued rewards. Those rewards are typically followed with most worthy year-end, bonuses for those above and beyond, over-extended efforts as displayed by the entire Sales Team. Believe me, Management and Corporate Executives *do notice those efforts;* and they all know and agree, *that nothing moves, until some one sells something!*

Getting back to the *MBO, Action-Plan* itself, we have already discussed how you determine the dollar amount necessary for your next year's **Goal** of Annual Gross Sales for 2010.

MBO-Objectives, you need to determine what *Objectives* you must achieve, in order to reach those *Goals* you set for 2010.

Again, the answers are in your 2009 Aging-Report. After performing your due-diligence, by comparing the *Gross Sales* results for all four quarters of 2009; you must review which Customer(s) are not reaching the *Goals* you set for their growth in 2009.

Then you determine which products each poor producing Customer is not selling. Next, you meet with all respective *Decision-Makers* for each of those poor producing Customers to discuss in-depth as to what they perceive as the problems causing their slow sales. You want these meetings to be amicable and productive, no attitudes allowed!

After gathering their valuable input, you discuss what the needs, in the way of healthy growth are for your Manufacturing Company, and why. You must ensure these Customers understand the concept of, *no growth; that is, no healthy growth, no profitable growth, creates stagnancy; stagnancy, or flat sales, means closing the doors of a Manufacturer. This is absolutely not an acceptable choice!*

Therefore, you must determine if it's the product that's not right for the area where this Customer is located. If this is the case, you can help them by switching out the products they chose to display and give them suggestions, based upon your experience, with the variety of products available to choose from, which may be *better performers*, in the sense of moving, *more product* per month, given their respective territory.

If the problem is not attributed to displaying and selling the wrong product for the geographical area, a lot of Customers will tell you that there is too much competition with other stores selling our same products for less. And this Customer feels, this is because the competitor is getting a better pricing structure than they are receiving.

You'll hear this excuse quite often.

Then, you explain that their competitor buys 500% more product than their Company. This is why they receive a greater discount. However, there are other ways you may assist them in moving more product.

You, the Manufacturer, may offer them a *50/50 Co-op, Advertising program.* Where, you will split the cost of an advertisement from their Company, with your products in the ad; your products only! No other company's products to be sharing the same ad. Then you can match their cost with you paying one dollar, for every dollar they spend on this ad, provided it meets the requirements from your Marketing Department. They always have strict guidelines and criteria the advertisement must adhere to; then you can move forward.

There are still more opportunities for this Customer to acquire a lower purchasing price. Such as, upon review, you learned through your Aging-Report, that this Customer always pays in (45) forty-five days, from the date they receive your invoice. You can offer *an additional 3% discount* to their normal 50/10% discount by paying the *invoice in full, within (10) ten days of our shipping the product.* We can notify them with both, a telephone call from our shipping department, and fax a copy of the invoice to the Customer. The phone call will verify the fax was received, and there were no questions about the order.

You, as the Manufacturer's Sales-Rep, may also offer them a greater annual discount; depending upon how much more this Customer will commit to sell per year. Example: If they can produce 300% of their previous annual sales, you may offer them a 50/25/3% discount on all purchases. But, they must perform on a prorated, quarterly basis. You'll be reviewing each quarter's sales. If they fall short of the pre-agreed commitment, *they'll lose that discount for the rest of the year.*

So by reviewing your *Aging-Report* periodically, I preferred to review it first thing, every morning; like reading the morning newspaper. I could see any unexpected activity, negative or positive, by Customer, by product and by area/region on a daily basis and react accordingly.

This is where you acquire the necessary data for you to set your *Objectives* as needed, in order to achieve your Goals.

MBO-Missions are those initial priorities you must set and fulfill in order to move on toward accomplishing your next set of *Objectives.*

Depending upon your 2009 year-end results will determine the direction of your actions in preparing for 2010. Whether your results exceeded your 2009 forecasted Goal, or whether your results fell short of your 2009 forecasted Goal.

In this phase of the *MBO-Model*, you have the opportunity to review areas of your Company. Every department is fair game, if it holds any benefits to improving your annual gross sales. Such as the Marketing department; they may be able to improve their catalogues, brochures and mailers. Any of these changes may seem to be only incremental to you at first glance. However, even if every department was limited to only a small incremental contribution, when you combine them all together, you will have a significant result, in a positive manner.

This is what I mean by being pro-active. You must be the one to start the motion to Make It Happen! It all starts with one step at a time, but it must come from you. You cannot rely on anyone else; you cannot count on anyone else and you cannot control anyone else's actions.

As I said much earlier in this book; *if you want to know the future, look at your past. If you don't like what you see, you and only you, have the power to change it!*

Again, look at each department to see if they can do anything different that may assist you in a positive manner. Go and meet with the Manager of Research & Development. They may be on the brink of something new, or an improvement to an existing product the Marketplace is just waiting for. Possibly, a *first-blood* product, where your Company is the first to develop a unique product, no Competitive Manufacturing Company has even thought of to date.

Your Company would *corner-the-market,* for about two, maybe three years. Then everyone would have developed their version of your once, new and unique product. But, those are two to three years of added revenues going to your Company's bottom-line. It would be imperative for you to capitalize on those moments. Remember, *maximize your strengths and minimize your weaknesses!* And like wise, *capitalize on your Competitors weaknesses and minimize their strengths.* Your, Board of Directors, love these axioms.

Then, you would apply the same exercises you used in your first two phases, *the Goals and the Objectives phases,* only in a lesser degree. I don't mean a cursory over view, but rather in reviewing your four quarters *Aging-Reports,* look for any obvious, or drastic negative changes to all your Customers sales versus their discount structures. Also, keep an eye out for that *Special-Account.* Everyone has one. They make the most noise and the least amount of purchases. In most cases, it's economically efficient *to cut them,* but *first check Legal!*

ADEE

A more sophisticated Sales-Managers Model

This Sales Model is specifically designed to target *newly appointed Sales-Managers.* As in the design of the MBO Model, the ADEE Model is kept as a unique, basic Model. It is also intended to be used as mortar, in building the foundation blocks of your basic structure, or frame-work, for your new level of responsibility as Sales-Manager.

I'm sure you have all heard the old saying, *keep it simple, stupid!* Well, I've never been one to embrace the *stupid* aspect. However, to *keep it simple* is something you should place into your memory banks until it becomes second nature. This is how you will develop your new ADEE-Action-Plan, Sales-Model to be a more sophisticated model.

ADEE is an acronym for the four phases to this Model: Assessment, Development, Entry and Expansion, are the only four basic phases needed for the newly appointed Sales-Manager to become successful in the Stewardship of their *Direct & Independent Sales Staff.*

Within these responsibilities of setting and surpassing of Annual Gross Sales, are the Fiduciary responsibilities over-seeing the Annual Budget for each and every Sales-Personnel under your auspices. With a *keen eye on Expense Reports!*

The role of Sales-Manager includes the *Training & Mentoring* as you perceive the need arises. By now you should be well aware of the fact that no one Sales-Rep is the same as the other. You must keep a sharp eye out for their personal idiosyncrasies between them. One Rep's gold is another Reps Kryptonite. It is incumbent upon you to pick-up on these differences ASAP, as soon as possible. As, each individual requires, a special unique method of *Motivation*.

With some, it's all about money; others it's all about position & power. And with any luck, you will have those who are in it for the *Passion and challenges in the World of Sales*, those will be your *Super-Stars; I guarantee you!*

ADEE, Assessment

Once you have completed the development of the final end product, your ADEE, Action-Plan Sales-Model for the new year of 2010, you must submit it to all your Superiors. If you are a District, or Regional Sales-Manager, it must meet the approval of your Regional Vice President, the Senior Vice President of the Company, the CIO, CFO, COO and the CEO/President.

There are some Corporations that suffer from *OCB, Obsessive Compulsive Behavior*. Albeit rare, they *do exist in the Board of Directors* and are typically, under one's breath, called *Control Freaks*. But, they will demand to be included in the review of your ADEE, regardless of the fact, they are way over paid and have much higher responsibilities to the Corporation than reviewing a Sales-Model so far down the pecking order; just be prepared.

But no worries, when your, first two immediate Superiors give you the stamp of approval, they will protect you and your Sales-Model from any and all unacceptable intrusions from that time forward.

The Assessment Phase includes, but is not limited to these factors:

Due Diligence:

Competitive Analysis, within your, *like industry*. Consider all like products, pricing, Customer-Service, delivery time and quality.

In-Depth Study of the previous year's Aging-Report by each of the four quarters - Each Sales-Rep's year-end results in gross sales and profitability – Each Customer's total purchases in gross sales and profitability (*consider all discounts respectively, as they vary from one Customer to another*) based upon each product every Customer bought, through-out 2009.

Upon completion of the *Competitive Analysis process,* the results will disclose where your company is actually ranked against its Top-Five Competitors. Including, who, where and what your respective Strengths and Weaknesses are and why.

At the end of this exercise, you will know the future direction of your Company and what changes you must put in place, to better ensure your success, as well as any changes *in Key Personnel, Retail-List Pricing, plus new changes with the overall pricing/discount structure.*

Ideally, after completing the Assessment Phase of the Sales-Model, the resulting data you acquired is now at your disposal to assist you in the development of more specific Action-Plans, with uniquely designed discount structures. Custom designed to meet the needs of separate and very different Customers and *their target goals.*

By applying creative thinking, redesigning your Action-Plans, Discount Structures and the quantities needed to qualify for greater discounts, you will be able to develop a more level playing field for those smaller Mom & Pop sized stores, as well as, the Internet. Thereby, allowing more opportunities for your products to reach all levels of the Marketplace, rather than limiting them only to the big Box Stores, or National Chain Stores and large wholesalers.

Do not lose sight of the fact that those smaller Customers buy and sell less volume, but with much greater profit margins for you, the manufacturer. You can develop these smaller accounts to become more competitive. One method is by getting the smaller accounts to make a commitment to increase the number of sku's, or units purchased by year's end.

How? By giving them a greater discount for products purchased for displaying on their Showroom floor. It's a well known fact, the old saying, *you cannot sell it, if you don't display it,* is a truism. Therefore, giving a better *Display Discount* to the lesser volume Customer, will at least increase your opportunity for these accounts to move more product because they are displaying more product. You will still benefit by increasing the volume of more profitable products.

ADEE, Development

Remember, this *Development Phase* is where *you* develop the new Sales & Marketing tools for your Sales Representatives, in assisting them to become more motivated and supply them with a better offering of Sales/Marketing Tools.

*Educate them on the **80/20 rule**.* In most cases, it is as follows:

(1) 80% of your Annual Gross Sales is produced by approximately 20% of your customer base.

(2) 20% of your product offering provides you with approximately 80% of your Annual Gross Sales.

(3) 20% of your National Sales Personnel produces 80% of your Annual Gross Sales Revenue.

Now, the question is; How can these **80/20 Rules** be applied toward assisting the Sales-Reps increase the new years gross revenues?

Using **rule (1)** go back to your **Sales-Bible, the Aging-Report**, and review the buying habits of your 20% customer-base that produces 80% of your annual gross sales revenues.

Look for any significant differences, other than buying in volume which only guarantees the customer the potential for a greater percentage of profit. The only reason I say *potential*, is because the customer doesn't necessarily have to keep 100% of the profit.

In most cases, they will display the product at list pricing, and after a short discussion with the potential buyer, your customer will have a good feeling for how much, if any, they need to discount the list price in order to secure the sale. They'll still be able to hold on to approximately, 93% of their gross profit.

Putting aside the obvious, the advantage of volume buying, you want to study these customer's Marketing techniques and policies. Some times there's a customer that has a very good and positive relationship between the Buyer and your Sales-Rep. At times the Buyer's willing to share some positive Marketing techniques with your Sales-Rep.

The most common Marketing technique used as many as once per month is the 50/50 Co-op Advertising program. This is where the Sales-Rep's Customer wants to run a large advertisement in the monthly newspaper. Your Company's expense budget, not the Sales-Rep's, will set aside monies earmarked for the larger, loyal customers.

These monies are used to split the cost of a large Ad, up to 50%. But, there are guidelines which must be adhered to, as required by the Manager of the Marketing department. In addition, the Ads must not include any competitive products.

Rule (2), being that those 20% of the product line, which represent 80% of the revenue are true every year, you must examine everything about those products; from design, color(s), pricing, uniqueness within the industry, availability to cost of shipping, or it could be something as simple as the geographical location of their Showrooms displaying your products. After which, you try to clone any significant *positives* that you may apply to *any* other products in your offering.

Another area to look at, would be the Sales-Reps themselves. Take a hard look at where those Sales-Reps stand when compared to each other. Look past the volume of products and look into the profitability of those products sold, that make up the volume dollars. It could be a high volume, low profit product. But, it is providing a large contribution to the total combined annual gross sales. But, has your Company ever tried to raise the price, slowly on an incremental basis? Small steps could lead to *enhancing the bottom-line!*

Rule (3): We covered part of this area in the previous *Rule (2)*. When you have 20% of your national sales personnel producing 80% of your entire annual gross sales, something is wrong.

Either your subordinate Sales-Managers are not performing any training at all, or they are not educated on how to train their Sales-Reps, or they are just lazy and are letting the 80/20 law naturally provide only the minimum required for them to reach their respective new year's Forecast. I have known copious amounts of Sales-Managers who are both, lazy and uneducated, skate through their careers. They are not indigenous to any one region; they are alive and well in every region of the country.

If this is the case with your direct Sales-Reps, then you need to start traveling with them on their sales calls. The good performers only require you to visit their territory from one to two times per year; If only to wave the Corporate Flag to the Executive Decision-Makers at your Customer's headquarters.

For those poor-producing Sales-Reps, you are going to have to spend four days per visit. Studying their MO, or lack-there-of. Then you will have to visit and travel with them at least four times per year; this allows you to include meeting *their* customers so you can meet privately with them. This will allow the customer to speak candidly about the degree of service they have been receiving from your Sales-Rep. You must, of course, take their critiques with a grain of salt, depending upon the Sales-Rep. As you are already aware, some of them are their own worse enemy.

What you want to take away from this *Rule (3)* is to *capitalize on your strengths,* by cloning those positive work habits of your best producers, and *minimize your weaknesses,* by applying those positive work habits to the daily work ethic of your less producing Sales-Reps.

I am fully aware of there being no *I* in Team; however, it seems that Sales-Reps are extremely competitive and have their own agenda.

Now is when you take the compilation of all previous data results and write them down. From all the information gathered in your Assessment phase and combine it with the results gathered earlier in your Development phase.

You will now call for an in-person, group, Annual Sales-Meeting in your Corporate Headquarters. In addition too your National, or Regional Sales Team, you should include your VP of Sales & Marketing, your Senior Vice President, the CEO and the COO in this meeting. The Host Speaker will be the Vice President of Sales.

Another reason for including the VP of Sales is because they are the guiding force for all subordinate personnel; plus their valuable input and experience. In addition, all subordinate personnel fall under the auspices of their position.

The Buck stops here refers to the desk of the VP of Sales. As to the other Corporate Executives, they will be in attendance only when required to add input where and when necessary from their respective areas of expertise; including their opinions of the final end product. The formal *Action-Plans* must meet with their final approval before moving on to the **Entry Phase** of the *ADEE-Model*.

Keep in mind, this meeting will probably run from an 8:05pm, Sunday evening group dinner, to six days of intense, pro-active meetings; typically starting at 6:01am for breakfast, on to 11:16am breaking for lunch. All meetings would start again at 12:46pm and continue on through to 6:59pm, at which time there would be a break until 8:05pm for another group dinner. This would continue until Sunday morning, when all attendees would fly back home, and expected to use the following Monday morning to review all new tactics, Action-Plans and newly Created Sales Plans to Enter the Market, starting first thing on Tuesday morning at 6:59am.

So, ***Carpe' Diem, Seize the Day!*** *Capitalize on your Competitors weaknesses and maximize your Companies Strengths!*

ADEE, Entry

Before approaching, how you will enter the marketplace with the new *Action-Plan Models* for the new year of 2010, please review the following list of salient points to remember and maintain in your *MO*.

Obsolete products must be removed.

Soon, you'll be a Vet, you'll know who the 'Slow-Pay's, No-Pay's are, as well as where the bodies are buried. That's when you know, you really know your Business.

The national Aging-Report should also reveal the same data for you to use as a comparative. You simply, look at one Rep, say in Miami, Fl, and you compare the same product velocity, any product, or group of like products, to that of a Rep in Los Angeles, CA, and find out why the discrepancy exist.

Again, capitalize on what ever the higher producing Reps use in their Game-Plan so as to be a *Mentor* to the Rep, whose numbers for the same products are low, to improve their territories overall results. And Vice-a-Versa, it also, gives you an opportunity, to review and really scrutinize any *like products*, where more Reps are showing lower than acceptable results.

It may disclose a problem in manufacturing, or just the fact, that the basic design has completed its life-span. Then, you should be communicating with R&D for their New, more Efficient and Effective Products, designed to improve your Productivity, to replace all obsolete products and act quickly.

Pull out that Best Friend again, the good old Aging Reports. Here's where you'll analyze everything under a microscope. Look for those slow-pays, no-pays accounts. Clean them up!

Apply an in-depth, Competitive-Analysis. See, whose Products, are outselling your, *like* Products, and why? And then, where? Is it Design, Price, is it location? Is it the Competitor's Rep? Do they have some kind of special relationship? If it is the relationship, depending upon how long back it goes, there are several ways to combat it. You must find out ASAP!

Maybe, it's because the Rep is a relative to the "Buyer", at the Customer's Corporate Office? Or, maybe it's due your Rep's poor performance on this Account? Either way, depending upon the reason, you should be able to find that Competitors weaknesses.

Keep in mind, *Familiarity breeds Contempt*, as well as *Complacency*! Capitalize on those areas. But, always be Politically Correct. Remember to put the right spin on it. Let the Customer/Buyer think it was his idea to switch to your New & Improved Products. Either, because of our new designs, or perhaps you discovered a new incentive package, where a slight increase in their purchasing, allows them to a very rare discount package.

Point being, **be Pro-Active and be Creative**, if you think there is a limited amount of risk to take, but the returns out weigh the risks overwhelmingly, *run it by your boss*. But, *be ready to show them the 'Up-side' to the risk,* and then, if they give the *stamp of approval*, your risk is gone. All you can do is come out a winner! You've just created a guaranteed, annual increase over last year's numbers.

Increase the velocity of all Products, over the previous Year-End results in a healthy and profitable manner. Year-End results ending as *status quo, is never acceptable* for a new year.

Cutting Operating Cost(s) is always a top priority for all Sales-Manager. Find where all *lost revenues,* are slipping through the cracks between your floor-boards!

Search out anywhere you think the Company's monies are being lost. Look for *Redundancies,* in or out, of the office?

Any Free Lunches wasted on low producing Customers? Do your Sales-Reps Crisscross driving to their Customer calls? Inefficiency causes Ineffectiveness! Inefficiency results in small *Bottom-Lines* for the Board of Directors!

Dedicate yourself to finding a better way! Look inside your Industry through your Minds-Eye. Now, study its history, present status and its foreseeable future. When you believe you know all there is to know about your Industry, apply this theory; *Take the Substance of the past, combine it With the Light of the New and you will find a better way.* Being a creative thinker, you will undoubtedly find *more than one better way* to improve your Company.

To be a successful Manager, you must display Pro-Active Leadership, a great listener, empathy, the ability to place yourself in some one else's shoes, kindness and a great sense of humor.

If you work in an environment that lacks, that kind of Positive thinking Leadership, my heart goes out to you. You don't know what

You're missing. By comparison, you would think you had died and gone to Heaven. *It's that significant* to work in a happy work place.

This is why, Corporations look for the rare personality of an Entrepreneur, the Creative Spirit, who is by nature, a Natural Pro-Active thinker. These rare People, make great Leaders only because they have a natural instinct, to expect the unexpected at anytime, 24/7!

So, these *Thinkers,* always prepare contingency Action-Plans. You will find these Leaders, almost on a daily schedule, talking to the Department Head, of R&D, asking, what's coming down the pipe? How soon will this next new Product be ready to go from Prototype to full production?

Again, this type of Leader will get a feel for that *Date* from the Production Manager, and you will find them in a meeting with the head of Finance, for an idea of a new type of pricing structure. After which, he will take all that data to the Head of Marketing. In order to determine, how long it will take to receive enough Marketing Literature to launch the new Product Line?

Keep in mind, all the above is performed as a Contingency Plan, in preparation for the unknown date when it is needed. You know what I am talking about. These *dates* are impossible to foresee.

Those People who just go through life, placing one foot, after the other, without thought, as to, what else can we be doing? What else is the Competition doing? Be Pro-Active, be well prepared, with contingencies, be the Creative One, be that inspirational, Entrepreneurial Spirit, that always stays, at least one if not two moves ahead of everyone else. Including, ahead of your own Boss! I was, and there is no better feeling.

It was that kind of thinking that kept me #1, in Sales, in every Company I worked for, which ultimately led to my promotions. Then, when I looked in my rear-view mirror, I would see all that money following me. It never failed me!

Review of all previously listed text prior to entering marketplace.

Who are your Top five Competitive manufacturers of *Like,* Products?

What are the specific prices and discount structures, for those like products, and do those prices change, based upon which Account it is?

List the possibilities on how your Company can garner a greater Market-Share, from those Top five Competitors. Be Pro-Active, when attacking these five Competitors.

Capitalize upon their weaknesses, and minimize their Strengths! Maybe their *like* product is priced significantly higher, than your product. Point out the great amount of savings their Customer can earn. Extrapolate it out for at least one, to three years, based upon their number of historically placed orders. Of course, at the new low price, they may decide to share part of that savings with the Public, or End-User, thereby automatically increasing their Velocity.

Bring this to the attention of the Customer's Buyers. Emphasize the savings would be a considerable amount of pure profit, to add to their "Bottom-

Line" at year's end. Making it possible, to create, more Bonus monies, for the alert Buyer.

Determine, if any of these Top five Competitors, have any products, unique to that specific Competitor. Should this be the case, surreptitiously find a way to buy that unique, product and send it to your R&D Department, in order to see if it is possible for them, to produce a similar, looking product, without causing any Patent infringements and still be a viable, efficiently cost effective, competitively priced *like* Product to present before your Customers and Potential Customers, with a *significant percentage of savings*.

Compare your own Company's Marketing & Advertising Programs, to those of your Top five Competitors. Do you have, a *Co-op* advertising program, where your Company will give the Customer a 50/50 split, on the cost of "Print" ads, Radio, or Television ads?

This is a good program, as it shows your Company is willing to pay 50% of a Print ad, while your Customer is making a commitment to advertise your products, and is supporting that commitment by paying the other, 50%.

Naturally, they'd have to meet the necessary requirements of your Marketing Department. You wouldn't want to pay 50% of an ad, displaying your Competitors products, as well as yours, in the same ad. That's just bad business!

You might want to keep your ears open, when you are out in the field to the possibility of a proven successful Competitor Sales-Rep, who may be unhappy with the Company he is employed with. There may be some legal way, allowing them, to come and work at your Company.

Be sure to run these possibilities, by your legal department first, before **ever** approaching such a person and get your Company's legal Beagles, "Stamp of Approval." Do not make a move without it!

It is not a matter of, what if your new employee's old Company will sue you, or not. Consider it a *given* they **WILL sue you!** This is the most Litigious Society in the history of Mankind. Always remember, and never forget, if there is anything, that you may be in doubt of, you *must* **CALL YOUR LEGAL DEPARTMENT, FIRST!**

Confirm the Company's new Annual Target Goals with the immediate Superior. This assures you that everyone is on the same page, prior to starting your Creative Process.

During the Creative Process, is when, you, along with your immediate Superior in Sales, plus your Accounting Manager, Marketing Manager, Warehouse/Packaging and Shipping Managers, and your Customer Service Manager set up a meeting in Group. All parties concerned, must be in attendance, at all times! Absolutely, no exceptions!

The Company's results for the entire New Year are all based upon this Group, Creating & Developing the best Sales Models possible, requiring the input from each and every Department listed above, to be in full agreement, that at least one Model is capable of implementing.

Once, you and your Sales Superior have agreed upon the Target Goals set by the Board of Directors, then you both, may develop two scenarios to present the Group Meeting.

Now, it is up to each member in attendance to offer an opinion based upon their expertise within their respective department, if any, or all new Sales Models, are viable.

Keeping in mind, each respective department is, more than likely, looking out for their own rear-ends, plus the degree of risk, they will be exposed to, should the final proposal fall short of it's mark, by year's end. There is a lot at stake, for all participants, based upon this Meeting.

Each department head is already aware, the basic Rule of "Efficiency & Effectiveness," must apply! In order to be truly successful, this Model, must surpass all, anticipated Goals and Mandates expected by the Board of Directors.

Now that at this point in time, the Group, already knowing what is expected of them, by the Board. They will set their Agenda. The prioritization will be dictated by results of the data secured by all participants.

An example would be to create a New Competitive *like* product found to be needed in all four Regions, in order to be able to compete, *apples to apples*. But, it is up to the R&D department, to give the basic cost of this new product, after the cost of the Prototype is approved.

Then, the actual cost data of the product is determined by the Manufacturing and Production Control departments after completing testing. This New, data will represent the True Cost of the new product, once it is in full production.

Then, the Group will look at *all* other internal cost factors, such as; repackaging, shipping product in bulk, to the Company's main warehouses, versus, depending upon the Customer. The New Product may have to be repackaged and reshipped, in smaller quantities. Or, the Customer may be able to take direct shipment from your factory, to one, or more of their Distribution facilities.

The quantity ordered will dictate the Pricing, and or, any discounts developed by the Sales Department, based upon which Customer it is, how much business they provide, and especially, their payment history.

Other factors in creating the Pricing of the new product may come from Customer-Service input. Such as your Customer *a*, may be known as a *Slow-Pay* account. This will definitely affect that Customer's price for the same product, it will definitely be higher, than that of a Customer that pays, immediately upon delivery.

Other factors in determination of the pricing of the New Product would come from the Marketing Department, such as, Advertising, locally, regionally, nationally, or internationally. Plus photo-shoots, Special New Product Launches, Media-Packets, literature, and samples.

Other Pricing and Cost factors, come from your Finance and Accounting Departments, on a Need-to-Know basis. Where, Salaries, Bonuses, Budget Expense-Accounts and Commissions are factored into the pricing structure.

It is also incumbent upon the CFO, to factor into every, Annual Budget, such cost factors which are classified as, Highly Confidential, Need to Know Basis Only! Such as, Projections for the New Year:

ROI: Return on Investment
ROA: Return on Assets
ROE: Return on Equity
EBIT: Projected Net Earnings, Before Interest & Taxes.

A compilation of all these Factors, play an integral role in the determination of the past, present and future health of the Corporation. Once they have be included with the projected Annual Sales Goals, then the Proposal may be submitted to the Board of Directors for their review.

At the end of the day, all personnel who are responsible for the performance of any Superior personnel are actually directly responsible to the Board of Directors. Should there be Shares and Dividends involved, you will not only be responsible to the Board of Directors, but also must be Accountable to the FEC, Federal Exchange Commission.

Much earlier, I alluded to the basic fundamentals of all "Successful Businesses." The following areas should always be considered first and foremost, for all Management Personnel, including, the Senior Executives, CEO's, CFO's, CIO's, and all Department Heads, from Manufacturing, to Customer Service, Accounting, Sales, Marketing, Warehousing and Shipping.

These fundamentals are:

Continued generation of Cash Revenues and Cash Reserves.
Keeping all Operating Costs of Doing Business down.
Prioritization & Delegation of Duties & Responsibilities

The Velocity of Volume, in every aspect listed above. Plus, the Cash, Production, Inventory, Sales, Obsolete Product, Personnel, Monthly, Quarterly and Annual, Aging Reports, to Percentage of Growth, or Loss, in Annual Gross Sales Dollars, Net Dollars, EBIT-Earnings Before Interest and Taxes, by each Product, each Sales-Rep, each Regional VP, Territory and Region.

All Personnel listed above should be cognoscente of every aspect listed, at all times. If not, you will soon find yourself on that Proverbial, Slippery Slope, leading you right out the back door. This Data is absolutely necessary in order for every Leader, Departmental or Executive, to ensure success in every endeavor you pursue!

As a Corporate Executive you are obligated to dedicate your self to the provide healthy, profitable results, at the least yet reasonable, Cost of Operation, and complete Fiduciary Responsibility to the Board of Directors, at all times never compromising, with unquestionable Loyalty.

At this point in time, you, the Sales Manager, should already have created and developed the individual MBO-Action plans unique to each individual Sales-Rep, and each individual Independent-Sales Agent having already met with each one, face, to face. They must be crystal clear, that their respective MBO-Action Plans and Goals are ready for Implementation!

They are the ones who are out in the streets, with whom, you have entrusted to represent the Company, as Professionally, Trained, Class-Act, Leading Manufacturer in your Industry. So, be absolutely sure, they heard what you said. Allow me to restate; "What you said, is what they heard!" Regarding, as to what is required by each one of them, in order for them to collectively, achieve success, by year's end.

The culmination of those uniquely designed *MBO's* are the Sales Guides, Sales Tools, and Sales Methods, you created for them to Enter, the very Competitive Marketplace, on the first work day, of the New Year.

In addition, you had to leave your Executive, Strategic Planning meeting, and all those Executives in attendance, with assurances, that you have received all the necessary input from all Departments, mentioned earlier, in time for you to take their input into consideration.

At *all* times, while you developed your complete, and thorough, final analysis of your Strategic Sales Plan, prior to your finally submitting your Proposal, on how your Company can expect to be very successful by next year ends results. You must, feel 100% assured, and comfortable, you are ready with all the right answers, the Board of Directors will ask you.

A brief recap of topics discussed in previous chapters:
1. Down to Basics
2. Common Sense
3. Dress for Success
4. Success Breeds Success
5. Back's of Shoes
6. Perception is Everything
7. The "Minds-Eye"
8. Know of what you speak
9. Talk the Talk & Walk the Walk

10. Be Prepared, for Everything, 24/7

11. Contingency Plans

12. How to give a Speech

13. Qualifying your Audiences

14. Competitive Analysis

15. Maximize Competitor Weakness + Minimize the Strengths

16. Maximize your Strengths & Minimize your Weaknesses

17. Cold Calls

18. Daily Call Reports

19. Business Cards, never leave home without them

20. State of Mind-Leave home Completely unfettered, each day

21. Never Mistake *Kindness' for 'Weakness*!

22. The best Sales person is the one who listens more than speaks

23. Murphy's Law vs Johnson's law; Johnson thought Murphy was an Optimist!

24. Complacency, the old saying, *if it ain''t broke, don't fix it*, flies right in the face of healthy business practices. In business, *he who stands still, is certain, to be passed by*!

25. Less is More!

26. Efficiency & Effectiveness

27. Log-jam of Indecision

28. Poor Management & Under Financed

29. Always be Pro-Active

ADEE: Expansion Phase

The *Expansion phase* is probably the single greatest area when most Businesses fail! More failures occur in the *Small Business Community*. Why? Two reasons; *mismanagement and under financed*!

Mismanagement and under financed have been allowed to infect, one Company, after another! Border, to Border and Coast, to Coast, without distinction, between specific type of Industry, size of Industry, or, and this is surprising, how much wealth, they started out with. Including, the fact, that most of these Small Businesses appeared to be financially sound,

36

and typically coming off of, a very nice, uninterrupted, five to seven year, growth pattern.

At this point in time, most Small Businesses are usually feeling *Pretty Fat,* almost, *Bullet-Proof* and *Biting at the Bit,* with head held high, enjoying feelings, or Delusions of Grandeur.

Sadly, I have seen this image, too numerous times to count. With, the Board of Directors at each others throats. Causing such chaos to occur behind those thick, Auspicious, Mahogany, Board Room Doors.

When the *Board of Directors* looks toward a new year, it's more like, looking at the start, of a brand New Senate-Session. Each, and every Senator, wants their fair share of the *Pork!* How, can there be so many different, Agendas, unique to their respective States?

Now, this is where one of Newton's Laws, come into play. *For every Action, there is an equal, and opposite reaction, that will occur.* This is a *Truism,* proven in the Laws of Macro-Physics. I'm sure you're all asking how, does this come into play, within the Board Room?

By comparison, in the *Small Business Community,* one of the Board Members brings up the fact, that there are finally enough Monies, in the *Cash Reserve Fund,* that they, *the respective Board Member,* may finally be able to purchase new manufacturing equipment. Believe me, they'll be prepared with all the comparative reasons, and Production charts to support the need in Manufacturing.

Immediately, following the Board Member responsible for The Manufacturing Department, shuts his mouth; at least half, if not all, the other Board Members, will jump-up, trying to over-talk, and out-shout all the others, with their own agendas to their respective Departments re: R&D, Marketing, Shipping and office equipment.

They'll all be demanding how much their, Departments needs are more entitled for these monies. Enter Chaos, *true-colors, and long-memories!* The *ties are off, and the sleeves, are rolled-up!* Now, it sounds like a Senate meeting, when funding time comes around.

That's just the beginning of a single case, during an *Expansion Phase,* all Hell breaks loose. So, let's say, this Company is blessed with a Strong Chairman of the Board. More than likely, he would put an immediate stop to the meeting from moving forward, until cooler-heads prevail. Maybe, even to be continued in a few days.

This sounds like a proper action to take. But, based upon, what I have observed, over the last thirty years, are the following facts: What ever amount of time has been given, as a break to allow clearer heads to prevail at the next meeting, is no different than before. Why? Greed!

Realistically, when all other Board Members and other parties concerned, are taking their focus off their main Duties and Responsibilities from the growth of the Company to be moving forward by applying Management Strategies ensuring Healthy Growth of their Company, but instead, lost sight of their true Goals and the Stewardship as to why they were picked above other contenders, for a Prestigious Seat, on the Board of Directors.

These are the times that your Competition is just waiting for. While your Company's major decision makers are stuck, like a log jam, the Competition will pounce upon your major accounts, maximizing your weakness of indecisiveness!

I believe these were good people, or they wouldn't have been given such great responsibilities. But now, they're all making their *Battle-Plans for, their Fair-Share of the Pie,* before the next meeting. Meanwhile who's running the Store? I'll tell you who, the same people who'll later be used as Scapegoats, for making tough wrong decisions. Hard decisions, ASAP!

But the Decision-Makers weren't to be disturbed! They were making ready for Battle. Soon, more & more bad decisions were made in all departments, until it was too late to stop. Ship's sinking! Everyone's scrambling around, dusting off their resumes and jumping ship. All due to human natures chink in their armor, *GREED*! Could it have been prevented? Yes!

In addition to the *Log jam of in-decision,* there is another major cause of Small Business Failures; and that is being *under financed.* When the SBC-Owner, or Board of Directors look at the high degree of Velocity of their Products, their initial response, is to call a meeting. Main Topic: Expansion, how to keep up with the velocity of growth, in Sales. The Company is in a conundrum. The *more we sell,* the *more we must make.* The *more we make,* the *more we must sell.*

Here are the topics of discussion: We need to secure a larger manufacturing facility, more manufacturing equipment, more manufacturing personnel, more raw materials, plus all newly created ancillary costs, such as more Workman's Compensation Insurance, Health Benefits, paid holidays, Sick leave, more Sales personnel to keep the new, high Velocity of product Sales.

Less is more. In a lot of cases, the Owners should re-evaluate their customer-base. They should be analyzing, Efficiency & Effectiveness.

Other costs could include; higher taxes, at years end, more Company owned/leased vehicles, along with the necessary Auto Insurance coverage, accordingly. Then, a larger storage facility, or the possibility of having to at least, looking at the leasing of a larger Warehouse and the necessary additional labor costs, plus the greater cost to rent, or lease.

Keep in mind, the most costly personnel to cover for Workman's Compensation Insurance, is a Forklift-Driver; usually runs about, three hundred percent of perhaps, a Front-Desk Receptionist. At the end of the day, you will definitely be looking at a much greater *Cost of Doing Business* each month, and what ever percentage that increases the over all Operating Cost's, you will have to include that into your daily activities, and adjust those Financials accordingly. More Productivity, more Sales, Packaging, shipping costs, etc.

Then, after including all new necessary additions to Company Personnel, is the Office Equipment required by each Department in the Company; Computers, enhanced Software, new and improved telephone systems, as well as the higher cost for the newly expanded Telephone Services.

These are just some of the associated costs for any size of Expansion Program. Also, don't forget, there may still be additional costs, regarding a variety of Consultant Costs involved in almost every aspect of the process.

It goes back to, the more you do, the more you have to do.

In addition to the obvious considerations previously listed, you must take a very serious look at your existing *Middle-Management* and *Executive-Management.*

Is the *New & Improved Operation*, going to be just a little more than the existing Management-Staff is sufficiently qualified to control? It will be a much greater burden of daily responsibility and stress upon each one of them, compared to, when you were only a *Start-up* Company, five to seven years ago?

Here comes that *Value Consultant*. If you don't, spend that money wisely, re, the *Value Consultant* today, you will surely regret it tomorrow, when it's too late, and you'll be tripping over all those chickens, running around, without their heads.

Do you feel strong enough, about those same *Original Personnel*, to entrust the future of the entire *Growth-Process*, your New Operation, will have to face? It may be worth waiting another year, give you time to beef-up your cash revenues, and lower more operating costs.

Those are the two most popular reasons for failure, within the Small Business Community; #1-Under financed, and #2-is Mismanagement!

Therefore, when I list the letter *'E'*, *for the Expansion phase*, it is the strongest recommendation, listed in this Book. That *Expansion Phase* simply means: **Go right back to your original Phase One**, the *Assessment Phase*. Then, you take a hard look at those first three years of Business.

Scrutinize them, even harder, than you had done, during those same years while in operation. *You are no longer the same Company* you were, back in the day. Today, you have earned your place in the Industry of your Passion.

Now, you have the Professional Insight of a solid, and well seasoned, Entrepreneur. In this exciting new Expansion-Growth phase, you certainly won't be making those same mistakes you did in the past. Only, this time, they will be a new Hybrid version.

This Hybrid version was never visible before, because it didn't exist at your previous level. Now, you are at such greater heights, your vision will be much broader, from that of your past years. Keep in mind, your risks will be much greater!

Remember, *for every action, there is an equal, and opposite reaction, that will occur*. When you, or your Subordinates, make a poor judgment call, the repercussions will be so much greater. That negative effect, at the wrong time of the year, could damage your Company permanently, or quite possibly, put you in Chapter 11.

So, I repeat, when you reach that perceived, *Expansion-Phase*, be extremely cautious, and extremely selective, in the hiring of New Personnel; mainly, your Middle-Management and Executive-Management personnel. Also, *be as judicious, as possible* in your spending monies on all those new Capital Assets, or you won't have enough left for your monthly Operating Capital.

Be cautious of not placing any undue burdens upon your new growth. Be aggressively conservative; especially with the Sales Personnel. They have to go out there, totally unfettered! They must be in the most positive frame of Mind as possible. They must be Pro-Active!

A brief synopsis of the "ADEE-Action Model," is as follows:

'A' , is for the Assessment Phase of the Model
'D', is for the Development Phase of the Model
'E', is for the Entry Phase of the Model
'E', is for the Expansion Phase of the Model

Which, is only listed as a means of communicating to the Owner, when they have reached the point, where they believe their Company, *may* be ready to Expand.

Expansion, for any reason, means they are to return immediately, back to the *Assessment phase*, to begin a well disciplined, re-assessment of their new *Expansion Business Model*. Because, any and all factors, that are of any significance, are now, entirely different than they had been, during the *Start-up Phase*, of the original Business Model.

Pearls of Wisdom & Tools of the Trade

- ***Nothing moves until somebody sells something!***

- *Dress for Success*. Success breeds Success!

- *Listen and learn* from all interactions, whether it's, one on one, or in a group meetings.

- Every morning, after waking up, look into the mirror and say to your self, *this could be the last day of your life*. What ever you do on that day, live it to the fullest, make it worth your while. *As you well know, one day, it will be your last!*

- Have a *pre-set schedule* for that entire day. For all activities of the day, whether it is work, or social.

- We are all born with a natural intrinsic value of *Common Sense;* use it! It's easy to forget during your daily activities. *You must put it to memory,* so you may apply it without even thinking. This process takes about three months.

- After which, you will find by applying *Common Sense first*, in reviewing a problem, your day will seem much less confusing and much quicker in *prioritization of your duties*. Simplify your problems into separate facets or categories.

- As a pre-requisite, all Leaders are required to know the first two Laws of leadership: *Prioritization & Delegation*. These are required at every level of leadership from Manager to CEO! You delegate to your subordinates those areas you believe they can handle; those duties far to costly to the company for you to be spending your valuable, hands-on, time.

NOTES

- *Perception is everything!* If you dress, speak and act as a leader; carrying yourself as a Professional Representative of a Successful, Industry; you shall be perceived as such. But, keep in mind, the opposite is just as true.

- When ever you are perceived as a *Successful Professional*, whom ever you speak with, will be hanging on your every single word you say. After all, you'll exude confidence in every way. Because of that perception, be sure, when you *Talk the Talk*, you can *Walk the Walk*. Why, you ask? Because, *you will be challenged* and definitely, you *will be called on it!*

- You must *be prepared* to know everything there is to know, on whatever the specialty-topic of discussion you chose. If you *speak as a Professional* in that field, you had better be one. If not, then you and the Company you represent will loose all credibility with that customer. This is when, *every action has an equal and opposite re-action.* Believe me when I say, within twenty-four hours your entire Industry will know *you are a fraud, a Paper-Tiger!*

- Integrity. Never do, or say, anything that will compromise the integrity of the Company you represent, or yourself! If, your true Passion is in Sales, the fastest way to become *Persona non Gratis*, in Your own Industry, is by compromising your *Morals, Ethics and Integrity,* forever!

- If you are, one of those type of individuals, who *BS's about, anything and everything,* you won't last long in any industry. The *World of Sales* has changed and there is no more room for those *Suede-Shoe/Snake oil sales people.* You cost the *Bottom-Line* and your Company's image, too much to cover anymore. There comes a time when you're knocked down, to stay down; this is one of them.

NOTES

- Actions, always, speak louder than words!

- *Maximize* your Strengths, and *Minimize*, your weaknesses.

- The same Axiom applies to your Competition; always look to *Minimize* their Strengths and *Capitalize* on their Weaknesses.

- Speeches. Be thorough, but keep them as short as possible. Pre-qualify your audience and, remember this basic rule:

  > First, you tell them what you are going to tell them about.
  > Then, you tell them about it.
  > Then, you tell them what you just told them, your recap.
  > From simplistic format, you extrapolate accordingly.

- *Never mistake kindness for weakness*! This is more about your perception of your Boss; but it also applies to customers and competitors. You'll only make that mistake once about your Boss.

- Personally, *I am* exactly that type of Leader. One, who may be perceived as a very nice guy, easy to talk to, and always ready to listen to anyone. I study when I listen to both positive and negative suggestions. No one is perfect. We all have our blind-spots, I respect and embrace the *Constructive Criticism* concept. I believe that constructive criticism should be a prerequisite for great leadership.

- Reports: Always keep your *Daily* Call Reports and Expense Reports current; and be sure to submit them on time! Always save a personal copy for your own records. Keeping a copy of both reports, have literally, saved the Company's and my own rear-end, in Courts over the last thirty years. Along with your normal scope of duties and responsibilities, come Depositions. It's part of doing business, so be pro-active by being prepared. Keep your records current!

NOTES

- I have been in over twenty five Depositions, during my thirty years. In a Court of Law, it is the person, who has their *dated notes* of the discrepancy in question kept in writing, who wins the Courts favor. All the rest is, *He said, She said,* to the Courts.

- Business Cards: As mentioned earlier, I cannot emphasize this enough; *always be prepared*! Always carry more cards than you believe you would ever need for that day. It's considered to be a *Cardinal Sin,* to be caught without one. Especially in front of your Boss. I've seen many Sales-Reps fired, right on the spot for it.

- If you want to stay on the good side of your Customers, always remember *the Golden Rule.* You treat your Customer, when he is sitting on his side of the desk, exactly as you would like to be treated, if *you* were in his place. In other words, don't tell your Customer, any half-truths, or blatant lies, if you don't want people to do the same to you, when you're in their shoes.

- The two *E's* every Leader should know!

    Efficiency & Effectiveness; what are their differences?
    Efficiency: Is doing things *right*!
    Effectiveness: Is doing the *right* things!

    Both need to be at their optimum level, in order to even consider, achieving *maximum Success.*

- I'm sure you have all heard the famous quote: *Revenge, is always best served, cold.* Where as, Confucius say: *He who seeks Revenge, best dig two graves!* I know the latter, to be very true, from experience. *When you harbor bitterness, Happiness will dock itself, elsewhere.*

NOTES

- Success: Everyone should know by now, that *Success is in the Journey* and not something you achieve upon reaching your Goals in life. Everyone wants to live on top of the Mountain *but true happiness and growth occur while you are climbing that mountain.*

- Remember the 80/20 Rule. It's a great place to find areas in need of expansion, or just more attention, thereby, increasing your *Annual Gross Sales.*

- The most expedient method of growing, as a person, is to surround yourself with people smarter than yourself.

- Opportunities are never lost. Why not? Because, there is always someone else close by, to grab the ones you miss.

- Whether, or not, your Company is the true Leader of your Industry, or not. You are carrying their Banner. So walk tall and carry yourself as you would, if your Company *is #1*! As long as you continue to do so, you will always be perceived as a *Class Act;* in time, you shall be!

- *Perception is Everything!* You walk, talk, and act like a *Corporate Executive* and you will be treated in kind. No matter what level you are in the *Pecking Order,* they will be hanging on your every word!

- You should always exemplify all the *Professionalism, and Integrity,* your Company is known for in their Industry. *First Class, Top-Drawer! Leader of your Industry!*

- Allow me to address, *Dress Code.* I am not saying, every sales-call should be made, dressed in a full three-piece suit; but certainly, no less than *proper Business Casual, Attire. Business Casual* is a Sport Coat, typically a Blue Blazer, Dress Slacks, Dress Shoes and a Dress Shirt. *A Tie* is a judgment call, based upon the Customer and of course, the weather. Ninety percent of the time, *wear the tie*!

NOTES

Basic Sales Etiquette

O k, now that you are dressed for Success; you must *always keep in the forefront of your mind,* how you look, act and speak, as if the CEO of your Company is in the audience. How you look, act and speak, should exude the highest degree of integrity, in representing your Company. *The most successful Sales-Reps are the best listeners!*

Like a Diplomat, representing the United States in a foreign country. Never compromise the reputation of the Company, for whom you represent. *Always the Gentleman or Lady, with the utmost respect and highest Integrity;* while consistently, maintaining oneself, as the consummate Professional.

When engaging in conversation, no matter where you are, *surly language is never acceptable,* no matter how your Customer speaks. *You never lower your Company's image* to that of your Customer. Maintain your Company's Integrity at all times!

Should your Customer choose to share some off-color joke; *it's at your discretion,* whether, or not, to *laugh with them,* or inform them that you are uncomfortable with that kind of humor and feel *it's inappropriate in a Professional Business environment.*

They say *Actions speak louder than words.* I don't know how to improve on that statement. Other Business Executives like myself, in an Executive capacity, have released many a Sales-Reps, Middle-Managers, and Vice-Presidents, for inappropriate actions and or, illegal activities.

Some actions may *not be illegal*, and yet, are *certainly never acceptable behavior* in any work environment. Such as: sexual-harassment, pilferage, hiring illegal-immigrants, etc.

Negative Sales: *Negative Selling*, by telling a potential customer, that your *Competitor is selling them inferior product*, or that the *Competitor's products do not meet the minimum acceptable standards* for their respective Industry. No matter how much greater your Competitors sales are compared to you, is never a reason, much less, an excuse, to compromise your personal morals and ethics by lying.

You will be discovered at some point in time. When this does occur, *and it will*, it will not only place a *well-deserved stain upon your personal reputation*, but it may cause such a negative ripple-effect, as *to result in irreparable damage to the Company you were representing* at the time. *These negative work habits are never acceptable* in the Business Community. Especially during such dire economic times as exist today, a Company will undoubtedly lose good Customers they held for several years, forever

Some day, you will find yourself in a *negative situation*. This does not give you the right to *respond in kind*. You are above those types of tactics. *You never respond in a negative fashion!*

Even if the stories are true! It is never allowed, under any circumstance! You sell and respond *only in a positive manner, in all situations!* If you find yourself being tempted to lower yourself to their level; *think twice, but keep your mouth shut!* Better they think of you as deaf and dumb, *than anything less than a class act, representing an honorable Company of high-held Integrity, Morals and Ethics.* It is beneath you to be any less!

What ever negative perception you may believe about any Competitor, you can always put a *Positive-Spin* on it, if only to protect your own reputation. Example:

You may say; *your products* are manufactured right here, *in the good old USA,* (rather than tell a potential customer, that your Competitors are manufacturing *inferior products* offshore, in China).

List of possible Reports for a Novice Sales-Representative:

There are typically *four basic Reports* commonly used in Sales Departments by most *Manufacturing* companies.

First: Daily Call Reports.
Second: Expense Reports.
Third: Annual Aging Reports, the most important of all reports.
Fourth: Cold-Call Reports, a time to plant seeds. No seed, no harvest.

I will not include a copy, as there are generic forms available at most Office Supply Stores, or your company has its own proprietary forms, designed to suite their respective needs, re; all three forms.

All three *forms* hold a position of great importance to your company. The information they provide is invaluable to the company and should always considered highly *Company Confidential*. The sharing of any data within either of these reports with anyone outside of the company is a violation subject to immediate dismissal!

The Daily Call Report is disliked by all who are required to use it and more if they must submit them on a weekly basis. It's usually thought of as a waste of good time by most Sales-Reps. Most Reps believe, that same amount of *time* would be better spent by either, driving to the next sales call, or applied to good, *Face-time*, with their Customer's key decision makers. I've spent several years studying this issue, weighing positives and negatives on *both sides of the aisle*. The Sales-Reps do have a valid point as to that period of time being spent in a more proactive activity.

However, as I mentioned earlier, if your *Daily Call Report and* those notes enclosed, *may be used just once a year*, during a Civil Action, as *documentation supporting your company's position*, versus a costly, financially negative perception, in a Court of Law; that single isolated incident is worth all your Sales-Reps time necessary *to document what actually transpired* during your last visit to that Customer. The Courts will give more credence to *written notes versus, He said, She said!*

Expense Reports: Commonly known in the trenches as, *Creative Writing-101*. As with the *Daily Call Report* form *Expense Reports* are available in a generic form and are readily available at most Office Supply Stores. However, as mentioned earlier, your company may have designed a proprietary form for your use.

Now, I personally believe most Sales-Reps may have filed a report with one or two false expenses in your past years. But, I am also fully aware of the numerous times you either lose a receipt, or left a restaurant without keeping your copy and you don't remember until you're one hundred miles away. So, I believe over a twelve month period, that it all balances out. After all, you are not in the business of Sales to set-up your *expense report* as a stand alone, revenue producer.

When you first join a company, most companies will have you go through one, or two days of indoctrination. During these days you will be given a booklet with the Company's Policies and Procedures. It will cover specifically what is, or is not, an acceptable expenditure. Should you *ever* have a doubt as to a meal with a customer or a gift at Christmas time is appropriate, or acceptable, check immediately before spending the money with your Boss, or the CFO. The last thing you need at Christmas time is to hear that $300 dinner you took your best customer out for last night, would not be approved by your Boss. If it does happen, believe me, you won't do it twice!

I know that I refer to this statement often throughout this book, but use your *Common Sense.* Always do the right thing. If you feel some doubt, or have some question as to it being the *right thing*, back off, more times than not, you'll find out down the road, you were right to back off. It's a very rare moment I don't follow my *gut feeling* about anything. Especially when it comes to, spending the Company's money. For a successful journey in your Career, you don't want even one single smudge against your credibility, morals or ethics. Never!

Aging Reports: I said it once, and I'll say it again, *your Aging Report is your Bible*! If there is any information you want to know about how you are doing personally, just study the results of your Sales efforts in your Aging Report. First you look at your over all gross sales versus where you should be on a prorated basis.

Let's say, your sales in the State of California are down from where you should be at this date by 25%. You must determine if it is due to a specific Sales-Rep, or territory. Maybe you find out your Reps in N. California are 15% over their prorated forecast. That tells you that if the combined efforts in California are down by 25% and you know the Northern California sales are up 15%, using basic deductive reasoning tells you that Southern California Reps are down by a total of 40%.

Now, you must examine by each Sales Rep in S. CA. If you find two out of four of your S. CA Sales-Reps are at 100% of their prorated forecast. That means your other two S. CA Reps are the main reason why California is down 40%! Now, you have to look at their customer base; who is buying, or better yet, who is not buying and why aren't they buying? You have to travel with those Reps for a minimum of two weeks. Calling on all their accounts not just their Key accounts but also their smallest producers. It could be inferior product, poor packaging, bad shipping, or just plain poor Service! You must find out why & make hard and serious decisions to change. It is imperative to include your Customer's input during the process.

After you feel you have the proper Action-Plan, to turn the S. CA territory around; first run it by your peers and then the Boss for approval. It may just require pouring more funds from advertising that was to be spread equally amongst your Region that given the circumstances must now be targeted to assist boosting your recovery efforts in S. CA. You may even find out that personnel changes are in order. What ever the reason, you must take immediate action in correcting those numbers. Because, your Boss is going to expect it!

Aging Reports, continued: It also contains all the information you need in determining your profitability and not just *Gross Sales*. As an example; the previous page discussed how poorly S. CA was performing, based *only* upon *Gross Sales*.

Although, S. CA is down 40% from their prorated forecast, this is only one of three categories you should *always* be tracking daily basis. Those three categories are: *Gross Sales vs Forecast, Net profit from those sales* and *quantities of all products sold*, by SKU, the bar-coded number assigned to every single product brought into your facility.

If you look further into the specific products sold by S. CA, you may find that they are low in quantities by units sold; however, they may possess the highest percentage of Net Profits out of all products offered in your entire offering.

In which case, although they are *down 40% in gross sales* and *number of products sold*, they could still be *15% over the forecasted Net dollars*. So, any ideas of firing anyone, is to soon to determine as yet.

This is where your *Sales-Management* skills come into play. Or, if you are not yet in Management, how *you go about* improving this situation may well place you in contention for a possible promotion.

It is now incumbent upon you to sit down with all personnel involved, and try to ferret-out an *Action-Plan* that will *kick-start* the sales of these *slower moving products*. It's a situation by situation type of problem, so consider *all things*: Co-op advertising, annual-rebates, additional yet reasonable discounts available *based upon performance only*. Such as: an additional 10% discount, on those slower-moving products, if the customer can increase the number of SKU's by 25% within the next 30 days. If this incentive program is a success, then it may be offered on a 60, or 90 day program. The amount of discount offered as incentive will be directly effected by the previous programs performance.

Cold-Call Reports: Some times you won't have preset appointments. Instead, you will fill your time with good old fashion *Cold-Calls*. Be brief, (5-10 minutes at most.) Remember, you had no appointment, so treat the Receptionist, (*the Gate-Keeper*) like a Queen. They can be your best friend, or your worse nightmare in that company. Try to get their birthday or anniversary date-of-hire with the company and *always follow-up* with *hand written* thank you cards.

This is an opportunity for you, personally, to plant the very first seed of interest, into the mind of the potential customer. Any actual Sales produced from Cold-Calls are a demonstration to Management, that *you can Sell*! That you can plant the seed, follow-up, nurture the account, and bring it to fruition, or *Close the Deal*, all on your own!

Cold-Calls are both, great challenges and great opportunities! I know from personal experience that a good Sales-Rep can average fourteen Cold-Calls per day, during the last three days of each month. That totals, forty-two Cold Calls per month and I would not accept *any less than 25%-33%* to become viable Customers. The Industry Standard success-rate averages 5%-10%. But who wants to settle for average?

A Professional Sales-Rep prepares in advance. The day before, you will have *confirmed all* preset meetings, *lined-up all* Cold-Calls, *double-check your amount* of brochures, catalogues, samples and business cards. A true Professional exudes Success, when ever they walk into a room.

It's a state of Mind! Success breeds Success. You have to leave home every morning with a positive attitude. When you leave your home each morning you must be *totally unfettered! Look ahead*! See the entire day, before it happens! *Picture the success*! At the end of the day, *you will have secured* a predetermined amount of new customers, Purchase Orders, or Cold Calls! *Picture it happening* in your *Minds Eye*, then, *Make It Happen! Carpe' Diem!*

The Close

Section One

In closing, I want clarify for you the reader, exactly why I wrote this book. I thought some of you may have lost sight of these two basic reasons, after having gone through the previous thirteen chapters; some what of a recap.

Ruth Stafford Peale once said, *Find a need and fill it.* Not many people know, her quotation has played the role as my own personal weather vane through out my life's vocation; the *World of Sales.*

I found *a need* for two separate types of people. Through so many years of travel I came across some of the unhappiest people I though could ever exist. After recognizing these people, I started to study them during my normal work duties.

It seems that most of these people got stuck in a career, much less a job that was originally only intended to be a temporary solution, to a temporary, negative financial problem.

Then, after a year, or two and getting caught-up with their bills and having saved-up a little bit of savings; they felt that false sense of security that most people feel. Now that they are current with their credit-cards, paying their rent on time for the last twelve straight months and managed to save about $3,000 over the last year. They feel pretty good about life in general.

However, this is that false sense of security I mentioned earlier. This is the perfect time for these individuals to pursue that career they felt so passionate about. After all, they only took that first job, as a temporary answer to a temporary negative situation. Now they can pursue their heart's dream; maybe it was the Fashion Industry, but given the sense of financial urgency, they could only get a job as a Grocery-Clerk to pay their bills.

Well, now they're at the crossroads when your mind plays tricks on you. Yes, they're now financially stable and if they stay with their present job, in another twelve months, their savings account could reach the necessary six months reserve, everybody should have as their *back-door, or rainy day* fund. However, beware. Why?

If you had a plan two years ago, you wouldn't have to ask why. But I haven't met anyone yet, who even had a basic life's plan. So, getting back to where the person is today. I'm sure if they've been a good worker, they may be looking at a promotion of some kind. Then, I'm just as sure, their little car, albeit paid for, is starting to look and act dated.

I think you can see where this is going. That person will settle for a somewhat comfortable life-style and probably go into a little bit of debt for a slightly used car, still ten years newer than their last one. And so it goes year, after year, after year. Before you know it, it's too late and you can't get out. Now, you have just qualified as one of the 57% who are unhappy in their present job.

That is the reason why I wrote the chapter on *Passion*. As I stated in that chapter, in the year 2000, 65% of the people in the workplace were happy in their job. But, a mere ten years later, only 43% are happy in their job. I believe the case I just cited is what occurs most of the time. And the numbers apparently validate my theory.

Pursuing your true *Passion* in life can be started at any point in time during your life. You do not have to stay unhappy day in and day out!

Granted, it won't be easy, but it's not impossible. Sure, you'll probably have to change your present life-style for awhile, but it will be worth it. I know, because I have been there. It took me fifteen years to make my way into the *World of Sales*. I saw my first sunrise and I never looked back!

When ever you decide to make that change for yourself, your life will seem like a dream by comparison to your past. There is no other feeling than being happy in your work. When you work in the field of your *Passion*, you actually can't wait to get to work. Use your *Mind's Eye;* picture being happy at work all day, everyday! Make it happen!

I know, if you haven't made that move yet, you'll find that almost too hard to swallow; but it's absolutely true. So first, make your plan. Then, make your move the sooner the better! Remember the old saying: *If you want to know the future, just look at your past. You and only you, have the power to change it!* Don't worry, be happy!

The Close

The second reason I had for writing: *A Better Way?* This title came from a quotation by Harvard Professor, Dr. Joshua Leibman, Dean of Harvard's School of Business, 1949.

Dr. Leibman, wrote a book titled: *Piece of Mind* in 1949. The focus of his book was about *Man's unending search for a better way.* I first read this book in 1982 for the first time. I have since referred to this book about every three to four years. Each time I read it, I discover another *gem* I hadn't seen before. I believe that I had to experience life more in order to read between the lines.

The greatest *find* I have discovered in the entire book, approximately 105 pages, is the following statement:

To take the substance from the Past and combine it with the light of the New and you will have a better way.

I have found this to be the answer to over 70% of the problematic situations over the last thirty years.

Who could make use of this single statement more than anyone else in the Sales Industry and when should it be introduced to them?

The answer I found to be, the sooner the better. It should be introduced to as their Mantra in the early days of their training. It has been mine for thirty years. So, the Novice Sales-Rep would benefit the greatest.

However, the next individual to benefit the most would be the newly promoted Sales-Manager. A combination of the two would be the best of both worlds, based upon potential productivity.

What I observed, between the years of 1980, through 2010, was an obvious, and growing, lack of educated Sales-Reps.

I do not mean that these Sales-Reps I observed were totally, uneducated individuals. I believe, most had earned a High School Diploma and had attended some College. Perhaps, even a small amount had earned, either, a two year, or a four year College Degree.

It was never about the amount of schooling, or education, they had received. It was about the specific lack of education applied toward their chosen profession in the *World of Sales*.

What I had observed was the complete lack of education in the world of Professional Sales-Skills or, the studying of Professional Sales Management Skills.

What I had originally interpreted as, the *exception*, turned out to be, the *Rule*. At first, I thought *shame on those Sales-Reps*, but that was not the case. At first, I thought all Sales-Reps were obligated to the Company, for whom they worked to at least study some basic *Self-improvement books* for their own purposes and their company would receive the benefits as a bi-product. Boy was I off on that premise!

Then I thought, where is the Sales-Manager; or where is the Boss, the Owner of this Small Business operation? These two individuals share the greater share of the burden of obligation. When it comes to the responsibility of *healthy growth in Annual-Sales*, the burden falls on the shoulders of these two key personnel. *That is* there main responsibility, to grow healthy revenues.

Still, that doesn't give the Sales-Rep any free passes, to do only the bare minimum to get by in their performance. The Sales-Rep has a responsibility to their Employer, to give 110% performance to improve the state of the company by doing all they can, *on and off* the job including self-improvement by Home-Study every opportunity that presents itself.

Their future is based directly on the healthy growth of their Employer's company. They are required to apply their absolute best performance possible as an integral part of each year's new Business Plan! But again, if your, (Sales-Manager's), subordinates are not performing at an acceptable level and I, as your superior, the Vice President of Sales for your region, would be found irresponsible by my superiors for allowing you, the Sales-Manager, to let your Sales-Reps flounder about in some haphazard, inadequate manner.

So basically, if *you*, as the Sales-Manager do not train, mentor and lead your Sales-Reps to successfully achieving your monthly and quarterly Sales-Forecasts, then I could lose my job. Believe me, you'll be history well before anyone starts to look at me. So you best start preparing an *Action-Plan* that will ensure you and your subordinates know exactly what is expected of your Sales team.

This book is not intended to include everything you should ever know on how to be exceedingly successful; so as to reach the level of Senior Vice President of the Corporation & COO. But rather, it is intended to be your *Basic Guide*, focusing you on learning *the basic formulas* in *Structured Sales Skills* enough for you to reach a point where you may supplement the original *structured formulas* with new ideas of your own. Ideas aimed at expanding your sales through healthy growth, so as to benefit your top three priorities.

Such priorities so as to, benefit your Customers, your Superiors and your own self-worth. I do expect that when you have completed this book and put it into practice in the real world, out in the field for a period of time, no less than three to six months, you will have broadened your scope of vision enough to foresee *potential problems*.

Given this new ability, you will be able to focus your energies, without hesitation, toward the most productive areas for you to best use your time. Time and motion, are key ingredients to any successful Sales-Rep, Sales-Manager and all Executives. These benefits all stem from reaching the pinnacle of *Prioritization,* one of the two pre-requisites of successful executive leadership; *Delegation* being the second of the two.

It is this same place in time when you have a firm grasp on, where, when and how, to best focus your time and energies that you may now, work on how to move up to the next level. That level of having convinced your superiors that you are now ready for serious consideration of a *promotion*. That includes the added *Duties and Responsibilities* that come with the new position.

Keep in mind, all this: having broadened your scope of vision, thus giving you the newly acquired insight to foresee *Potential Problems,* which we call *Anticipation*. When you can anticipate a potential problem area, puts you a full step ahead of the Competition and perhaps your own peers. This ability saves the company time and saving time is saving unnecessary spending of revenue. It's all good! Very good!

None of this would, or could ever have happened without you having learned the basic structured Sales-Skills to the point where you no longer have to consciously think about those steps. They have become second nature to your thought process. You *must learn the basics* in order to grow.

This brings you to the initial basic lessons of the *next level;* the two E's. *Efficiency and Effectiveness!* The greatest significance being; what are the basic differences between the two? Hearing the difference is one thing; then it is obvious.

Efficiency is doing things right,

Versus

Effectiveness is doing the right things!

I know, it sounds extremely simple. However, the application of this rule plays a great role in your entire process of developing and implementing a new and different style of designing your next year's *Annual Gross Sales Forecast*. Because, once you have signed-off on that proposal and submit it to the Executive Brain-trust, there is no taking it back. This group is going to go through that Forecast with a fine tooth comb.

They are going to want to know *what* you are going to do for next year, *where* you plan to exact your greatest efforts, *why* you are going to do it there, *who* you are going to make this happen; who are your Super-stars going to be and *how* it all comes together, in concert in order for you to achieve that new Forecast. Why do they want to know every little aspect of your new year's Action-Plan?

Because, they have to walk in and put it into the Board of Director's hands; and they will have to be able to come up with all the answers; the answers that you gave them to substantiate the new Budget required for them to achieve your new Forecast, in detail.

So, back to the differences of Efficiency & Effectiveness; obviously you don't want to expend your staff's energies of doing the *Right* things, if you're not going to do things *Right*, or correctly. It would be just as big a waste of time as doing things *Right*, or correctly, if you wasted your time doing it on the *wrong* things.

Your customer's are expecting you to present them with something that will give them the most *Bang, for the Buck!*

How will this be possible, if you cannot apply the rule of the two E's to your new *Action-Plan*, thereby giving your own company their most *Bank for the Buck* by applying the highest degree of Efficiency & Effectiveness in every aspect of your *Development phase* of your new year's plan; then you have failed your Company and your customer

Obviously, all the above will take some time to learn before you are able to put it into practice in the development of solid *Action-Plans* for the Sales personnel and into the creation of a *healthy, fiduciary-responsible, Long-term Strategic-Plan*, so as to co-inside in concert with the Executive level's *Short-term and Long-term Strategic Plan*.

As you can now see, you cannot get here, from there, without first learning the basics. The lessons in this book should help you accomplish that first Mission. From that point on will depend solely on how serious you are at becoming successful in the World of Sales.

These last few pages will give you some blank outline pages for you to practice with, using your own information from your own Aging reports, showing you where you must focus, on what products, which personnel, by what products/services and which customers and against which competitors.

Remember, the *Bottom-line* dictates all! Your value to the company is always based upon performance. I hope this book helps those of you who had no direction before. Because I firmly believe in order for us to get our Small Business Community back up to where it belongs, the Back-bone of the United States Economy, we have to start at the first rung of the Sales Ladder and also the newly appointed Sales Managers.

Small Business Owner's, consider the Gauntlet thrown down!

Outline Lessons for Your Exercise

MBO:

Management by Objectives.
(intended for new/first year Sales Representatives)

GOALS:

Realistic increased goals for Gross Sales
Net profit dollars
Customers and Key products

OBJECTIVES:

Specific areas determined to be at an unacceptable level and how you plan on improving them in order to reach the above Goals; be specific!

MISSIONS:

Complete a thorough investigation of your fourth quarter Aging Report to determine what basic Action-Plans you need in order to be able to accomplish your Objectives by order of prioritization.

Remember, your Aging-Report is your *Bible;* it contains *all the necessary data* you'll need to complete this Action-Plan.

NOTES

ADEE
Assessment • Development • Entry • Expansion

Assessment:

To proceed through this process, you will have to perform an in-depth due-diligence effort in your industry.

Again, first review your final Aging Report to see what areas are in need of serious review by territory, by Rep and by product.

This includes: Expense budgets, by each Sales-Rep. Are they over or under budget and by what percentage and why?

Look for any specific weak product velocity. It may be directly due to the poor support by the Rep with that single product. They may have a very good reason, or not. Also, check the age of the product. It may be that the life-span of this specific product has had a good run, but it is now considered, *Dated*.

Then look at each Sales-Rep's performance regarding reaching, passing or falling short of their Annual Forecast. A Sales-Rep who seems to be way off the mark, may or may not, have a good reason to support their respective standing.

NOTES

Competitive Analysis is Priority-1! Check with your closest customer's *Buyers* for any new *incentive plans*, or any new product launches to be expected, or may have already taken place by your competitors; check on as many *List-Price* changes, or any new *Discount-Programs* offered by your competition. Any of these factors may cost you this customer.

During the process of your due-diligence, you may want to check into any rumors of discontent by any of your own Sales-Reps. If so, sit down with them, (if they're worth it) and see if you can resolve these perceived differences. After all you invested lots of time and money in your best performers.

There is no *good* point in time for any company to *take the hit* of losing a good performer, in any position; from the warehouse personnel to the executive level.

It's a *Double-Whammy* if and when it occurs. First you lose that ongoing forward thrust in that specific area they held, along with all those strong, *Sales-Rep/Customer relationships* that took years to acquire their trust. Plus, you now have to cover for them until you can find a replacement.

When you do find a replacement, you still have to endure a period of time for the *Learning-Curve* to take place before they're ready to hit the streets. But, it's still the old *one step forward and two steps back* for about three good months.

NOTES

Development Phase:

To develop your Action-Plan for the New Year, Forecast included, you must gather *all* the relevant data you acquired during your *due-diligence Assessment* process and look at each facet of the entire compilation on a case by case situation; customer by customer, Rep by Rep and product by product. This data will dictate where and what changes are necessary in order to achieve *new healthy growth in revenue.*

Remember, this new Action-Plan must display very succinctly what changes you are making in the respective area of your responsibility. You cannot just tell your Sales-Manager your new years gross sales forecast will be increased by 20% over the previous year.

So be prepared to show, not only the specific changes you are making, but why you chose to make them and where you are making them. More than likely by Rep, by Customer and by product, including your Expense Budget; you must be able to support and defend all recommended changes to your Superiors, one by one.

But, be ready for some input such as, suggested changes to your Action-Plan; just remember it is not personal, these will be coming from more experienced personnel and should be taken as constructive criticism, but all in a positive nature for the good of the Company. After which, when you agree to agree, then submit the final version you developed for them.

NOTES

The Entry Phase:

This *Entry Phase* must be implemented as a group effort. It will require the attendance and interaction with no less than, the four Regional Sales-Managers, along with their respective Regional Vice-Presidents of Sales, with the Vice-President of Marketing, the CFO, Chief Financial Officer and the Senior Vice President/COO, Chief of Operations.

These executive staff members are necessary in order to know specifically what the parameters are in each of their respective areas of responsibility.

The four Regional Sales-Managers may believe they have the perfect Action-Plans for the New Year; only to find out that the CFO has been instructed by the Board of Directors, that their will be a maximum of 5% increase in the Marketing budget and a freeze on all Expense Budgets.

This is where you would all, in group, find out all products in the previous year's offering that were manufactured in Canada, are now adding an additional 3% increase in order to cover their delivery costs to your four regional warehouses.

In addition, you may learn at this group meeting that 20% of the previous year's product line has been determined obsolete; and R&D can only provide approximately 10% newly designed products to replace the obsolete 20%.

NOTES

After hearing the new information about Budgets, it's obvious that it's *back to the drawing board* for all the Regional Managers.

They will now have to change any new Marketing ideas to conform to the limited 5% increase. However, some portion of that loss will be helped out by the announcement from Manufacturing that 20% of the previous year's product offering is no longer available.

On that same note, it may be wise to dedicate those additional 5% Marketing dollars be used toward updating the company's catalogue and perhaps any advertising to be focused upon the new 10% product offerings.

The hardest part of entering the marketplace in the New Year, will be *Passing on* the 3% increase on all products brought in from Canada. Price increases are always hard to pass on.

You'll have about half of your long-time customer base that understands these types of things. It's all part of the ongoing costs of doing business. They understand when fuel prices jumped 25% that this will have a direct effect in everybody's freight costs, including their own and all your competitors.

NOTES

Entry Phase, continued

However, now *the Bell tolls for thee,* it's time to face the other half of your customer base, the one's that gripe if the Sun didn't come out that day. And believe me, they do exist!

How is this problem handled? I found the best way, especially with these kinds of personalities, is to meet with each and every one of them, face to face. *Mano a Mano!*

Although, I strongly suggest if any of these negative personalities are one of your larger accounts, you as the Regional Sales-Manager, should accompany your Sales-Rep on the Key-account calls. Because, they are going to make all kinds of threats, including dropping your line of products all together; 99% of the time they are just bluffing, but they will try to squeeze a larger discount out of you.

If the Sales-Rep were there alone, they would probably cave-in and just give them an additional 3% discount on everything they order throughout the year. But, as the much wiser Regional Sales-Manager knows better; the Regional can stop the customer's ranting by letting him think he is getting a 3% discount on all they buy through out the year.

NOTES

Realistically, the Regional Sales-Manager shall write-up a statement giving a 3% discount, in the form of an annual-rebate program where the customer must show a growth of at least 15% by years-end, in gross annual sales. This way, your company will make up that 3% in the additional 15% velocity in product sales. So, basically the customer gets his discount only based upon their performance. If they increase their annual sales by only 9%, then they do not qualify for the discount incentive. This method typically works more times than not, based upon my own experience.

As to those same negative personality accounts that are much smaller in purchasing power; that's when it's time for the Sales-Rep to *cut their teeth on*. That's how they learn; after all how did you think the *Regional* handles it so well; by lots of practice while they were basic Sales-Representatives.

So, after going back to the proverbial drawing-board and interacting between each other; it only takes about three to four more days of re-designing each other's Action-Plans with the assistance of the executive staff there to guide them along to fruition. Then the *new Action-Plans* now meeting all budget and manufacturing constraints, may be submitted confidently to the Board of Directors for approval. Then, you may send your Sales-Reps out with your new *Action-Plans*.

NOTES

The Expansion Phase:

When a company believes they are *bursting at the seams* with strong sales, a solid customer base, seasoned Sales-Reps, solid long-term relationships between all three parties concerned; the natural progression is to make a real strong commitment toward *Expansion*.

History proves that a great majority of the times a company implements an *Expansion phase,* they fail! It takes a great deal more internal scrutiny, along with an in-depth study far greater than was applied in the company's Start-up days.

Why? You've already achieved the level of a successful business operation. In the last three to five years you have been focused mostly upon growth for the sake of growth, or you would be passed by all your competitors.

Well, job well done; now you are looking to grow a very significant percentage in the size of your company. You have far more to risk than those early days of small investments, long hours, kissing a lot of frogs in Human Resources in order to have secured the professional executive and middle management staff you have today.

NOTES

In the process of your ongoing business, you've been getting all the positive signs from your customer base that is telling you, they will support your growth due to the fact that all Buyers know they must have a good mix of manufacturers to protect themselves.

However, in the ADEE, *Assessment, Development, Entry & Expansion Strategic-Plan,* I strongly suggest you stop any *Expansion* ideas immediately. I cannot emphasize enough about these warnings.

When companies enter into an *Expansion phase,* I am compelled to direct you to go back to your Assessment Phase immediately!

More companies get into so much trouble during this transition that chaos ensues and Customer-Service is trying to explain why their customer's products are late; soon becomes compounded by the pre-existing purchase orders for their products, but nobody took into account Manufacturing.

Manufacturing is trying to bring the newly designed products *on-line* for the New Year. Typically, this is an ordinary and uniform process. At least it was during the last three years, or so.

NOTES

Manufacturing has brought new products *on-line* before. Soon, you will have the *Blame-Game* with a lot of finger-pointing going on, but now there is a Purchase order/Manufacturing/shipping and irritated Sales-Rep *clog* in the natural flow of things you had prior to your new *Expansion-Phase*.

Mismanagement and under-financed, are the two main causes for the failure of Small Businesses in this country. The key-decision makers are so caught-up in the *concept* of expanding their operations, seeing the extrapolated numbers they never dreamed of in those early years and the new building-site for their combined operations and manufacturing; they lose sight of those same basics that they applied when they first started their company. You must start just as hard, no, much harder than you started in your first *Start-up days*.

In your *Assessment Phase* you have to look at your management-staff even harder this time. Are they savvy enough to bring their teams to those new heights which are necessary to satisfy the greater mandates by the Board of Directors? Are they capable enough to handle the greater duties, responsibilities and Stewardship so necessary for them to maintain the steady, healthy growth needed to succeed for this newly expanded and demanding, Company.

NOTES

Finale

The more you do, the more you have to do. The bigger the Monster you build, the more you have to feed it. So when you reach the *Expansion Phase* of your *Long-term Strategic- Plan,* don't make a single move, until you gather all Executive staff and middle-managers and go back to Phase-one of the ADEE Plan, the Assessment Phase and act like you're starting-up a new company all over again.

At this time, I would like to remind you the entire premise, as to why I wrote this book. *I found a need and filled it.*

I saw the Country's economy go right down the old toilet!

Who took the *brunt* of the pain in the Business Community?

Whose Business Representatives have the least amount of professional educational schooling, training or mentoring in the *Art of Sales?*

The answer is *the Small Business Community!*

I have incorporated the two most basic formulas to boost sales and added these two mantras to develop this book, so as to assist the *Small Business Community* regain its position as the *Backbone of this great Country.*

Mantra #1: *Take the Substance of the past & combine it with the light of the new and you will have **a Better Way!***

Mantra #2: *If you want to know the future, look at your past. If you don't like what you see, you and only you are capable of changing it!*

You cannot waste another day, read this book, or take my two day seminar and get started on recapturing your lost revenue!

About the Author

My background over the past thirty years includes having worked in a corp/exec capacity for five, multi-billion dollar manufacturing corporations in the World of Sales and the Art of Selling.

My PASSION, was always in the World of Sales. Specifically Mentoring & Training Direct & Independent-Agents, new to the Art of Selling! I've Mentored over 1,600 Sales-Reps. Several have gone on to become Entrepreneurs, Captains of Industry, or found their true passion at a specific level, perhaps as Senior Vice President of Sales; not aspiring to higher levels in the Corporate structure, as myself; in my last position as Corporate Executive, Senior Vice President.

I spent seven years with that organization taking it from $800,000 gross annual sales in the western region as their Sales Manager up to $10,500,000 within (18) months. I was then promoted to Western Regional Vice President of Sales; during which I took the western region annual gross sales from $10,500,000 up to $22,800,000 within the next

(12) months, representing 55% of the entire International gross sales. I was then promoted to Corporate Executive Vice President of the Company. I was directly responsible for (5) Vice-Presidents, 200 Sales Reps & over 600 Distributors. Shortly after I took total gross sales to $52 million. I was offered a promotion to President/CEO. I did'nt take it, I felt it required compromising my high standards of Morals & Ethics. Therefore, I was asked to leave the Company. I was happy to do so. When I left the Company it was at $62 million a year.

In the year 2000 I started up my own Consulting Co. , "Morgan Franklin Associates", a Sales Management Consulting firm, creating business plans for Start-up companies, Expansion-Divisions & Crisis Management. I traveled to 40 states, Canada, Mexico, Japan, China, Germany & Italy. After seeing the terrible declining economy, I realized who would be hit the hardest first, the Small Business Community. I felt compelled to help, or assist that segment of the Business Community any way I could.

In 2010 I decided to write this book. Spending two years of due-diligence, I deduced the quickest way to help, was to focus on the area that could help them recoup their losses, in the shortest amount of time. That is to "plant" the seeds in the newest most excited people in sales; the new Sales-Rep and recently promoted Sales-Managers. But both had to feel Passionate about Sales & never exposed to professional education in structured basic sales and strategic planning the founding Fore-Fathers did not create the Backbone of this great country, only to see it crash and burn!

I read an article written by an independent survey company stating, in 2000 there were 65% of the workforce that were Happy in their job. In 2010 there were only 43% happy in their jobs. The writing was on the wall, lack of Passion in the workforce!

I've committed a percentage of the profits of this book to be given to the Small Business Community, where I could see the most need.

Born: San Francisco, CA moved to Santa Clara before it became the heart of Silicon Valley. Formal study:Math-Bus. Architecture; Home Studied 25yrs through Harvard School of Business Mngmt, Prof & Dean,.Michael J. Porter & Dr. Deming's TQM+JIT Mngmt. concepts, the Art of War by Sun Tzu, Dr. Joshua Leibman's Peace of Mind,Harvard: Jack Welch-GE; David Schultz-IBM; Dr. Woods-Industrial Psychology & it's Social Function: Never Stop Self-Education!